# Railways
# of Keighley

### by
### J.M. Bairstow

Dalesman Books
1979

**£1.75**

The Dalesman Publishing Company Ltd.,
Clapham (via Lancaster), North Yorkshire

First published 1979
© J.M. Bairstow, 1979

ISBN: 0 85206 527 2

Printed by Galava Printing Co. Ltd.,
Hallam Road, Nelson, Lancs.

# Contents

The cover photographs show:- Front: Ivatt 2-6-2T No. 41241 approaching Haworth (J.M. Bairstow). Back, top: 'Claughton' No. 5932 hauling the 'Thames-Clyde Express' near Keighley about 1935 (Real photographs). Back, bottom: Train at Wilsden on May 21st, 1955, the last day of passenger services (Edgar W. Morrell).

Photographs in the text are on pages 25 - 32 and 49 - 56.

Maps by the author.

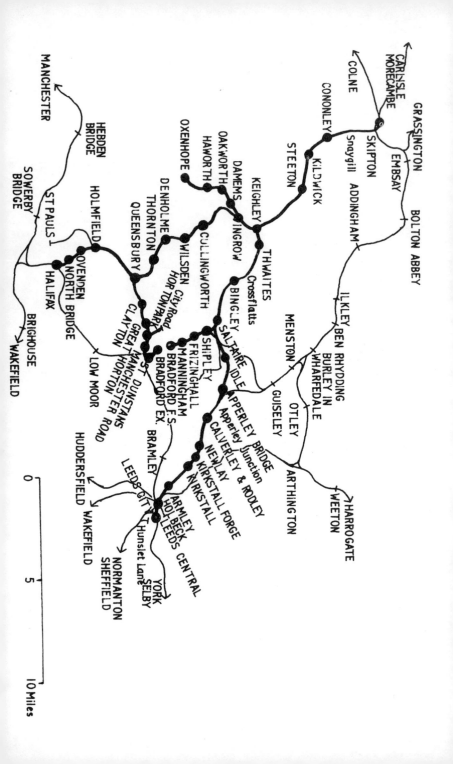

# Introduction

THE TOWN of Keighley is situated at the junction of the rivers Aire and Worth. The railway station which is the focal point of this book is found at the junction of the Aire Valley and Worth Valley lines.

The main line runs through the Aire Valley and is covered in chapters one and two. Keighley is served by trains from Leeds to Skipton, Carlisle and Morecambe. There is also a local service from Keighley to Bradford Forster Square. Nowadays this latter station is very run down, but when the railway was built it was the route from Leeds to Bradford which was the main line and the extension from Shipley to Keighley and Skipton was of secondary importance. Before considering the line to Keighley, we must see why the first railway from Leeds to Bradford took the circuitous route via Shipley and why the line was never extended beyond Forster Square, thereby explaining why Bradford remains to this day with two separate terminal stations. We can then follow the development of the line through the Aire Valley which later became part of the Midland main line to Scotland.

Chapter three is devoted to the Worth Valley branch which was built, like so many others, to serve the local textile industry but which also had from the start a tourist traffic. The arguments voiced against closure in the early sixties are considered together with the preservation scheme which revived the railway and developed its tourist potential.

So far Keighley is seen as a Midland Railway stronghold but in chapter four we consider the heavily engineered and expensive route by which the Great Northern Railway broke the Midland monopoly and also served, inconveniently in some cases, the intermediate villages which are now left without railway communication.

The story of Keighley's rail transport is completed in chapter five with a reference to the tramway system which consisted of only three route miles and which was the first municipal electric tramway undertaking in the country to be completely abandoned.

The main theme of this book is the development of the train services. Little detail is given of locomotive matters but Keighley was on a main line and was visited by most classes of the Midland Railway and its successors. The variety of motive power on the Great Northern Railway at Keighley was not so wide and the 'N1' class engines which appear in a number of the photographs were the mainstay of passenger services for a long period.

This work would not have been possible without the assistance of a number of people whose help I gratefully acknowledge. Mr Ralph Povey, the president of the Keighley & Worth Valley Railway Preservation Society, has given me access to some of the material upon which his own book on the K.W.V.R. was based. Were it not for Mr Povey and my other colleagues in the society, there would be less to write about anyway. Mrs Margaret Jones typed the manuscript. Mr Stuart Baker read it, offered suggestions and submitted photographs. Some of these, although taken in comparatively recent years, are already of historical interest. The photographic coverage of the Great Northern Railway would be rather bare but for the contributions of Messrs John Oxley and Roy Brook. It would have been impossible to include the chapter on the Keighley Tramways without the help of Mr Stanley King. I am indebted for the help and advice of Mr David Joy of the Dalesman Publishing Co. Ltd. and to the other photographers whose work is credited in the following pages.

# 1.  The Aire Valley Line

### From Construction until the Grouping

**Plans to link Leeds with Bradford**

Leeds first gained the benefit of railway communication when the Leeds & Selby Railway was opened on September 22nd, 1834 from its terminus at Marsh Lane in the east end of the city. Nearly six years later, on July 1st, 1840, the North Midland Railway completed its line from Derby to Leeds which was thereby placed at the end of a continuous railway route from London and the Midlands. The Leeds terminus was at Hunslet Lane, a mile from the city centre.

At this time Bradford was already established as the centre of the woollen industry but the best the railways could offer was a suffix 'for Bradford' in the name of Brighouse station, 6½ miles away and an hour's journey by road.

The distance from Leeds to Bradford is about nine miles. There were two routes by which a railway might be built. If a line followed the route of the canal via Shipley, the gradients would be easy, but the line would be four miles longer than the alternative via Stanningley. On the other hand the shorter route would be gained at the cost of 1 in 50 gradients.

Bradford business interests approached the North Midland Railway even before that company had completed its line to Leeds with proposals for an extension to Bradford. The North Midland indicated that it was fully occupied with its existing lines under construction and could not contemplate taking on further commitments. The engineer to the North Midland Railway was George Stephenson who advised the Bradford party to form their own company indicating that he would be prepared to act for them in his professional capacity.

Stephenson favoured the route via Shipley and carried out a survey in 1838. No progress was made until 1843 when a scheme to form a Leeds & Bradford Railway Company was put to Stephenson who obtained the support of the North Midland Railway and of George Hudson, M.P., a North Midland director.

The provisional committee of the Leeds & Bradford Railway held its first meeting on December 22nd, 1843. Hudson was elected chairman and John Waddingham of Leeds deputy chairman. On December 30th, the provisional committee met to allot shares. The public response had been so great as to oversubscribe for the number of shares available. Many applicants were allotted either no shares or only a small proportion of those applied for. Hudson and Waddingham on the other hand allotted to themselves £30,000 and £10,000 worth of shares respectively, almost the number for which they had applied. The total share capital was £400,000.

When the Leeds & Bradford Railway Bill came before Parliament, Bradford merchants told the committee that it cost as much to transport goods from Leeds to Bradford by road as it did from Hull to Leeds, five times the distance, by rail. Opposition came from the 'short line' party who favoured the route via Stanningley, but this was unsuccessful and the Bill received the royal assent on July 4th, 1844.

Immediately on receiving Parliamentary approval, work was commenced on the two major earthworks on the line, the ten-arch Apperley viaduct and the 1,496 yard long Thackley tunnel. Although the line followed the course of the river Aire most of the way from Leeds to Shipley, this tunnel was required to avoid the lengthy detour which the river takes through Esholt. In addition to Apperley viaduct, six bridges had to be provided over the river Aire and four over the Leeds & Liverpool Canal. These were all built in plain style. On February 20th, 1846 the directors were advised that about two-thirds of the track was laid, many bridges were completed and work on the tunnel was at an advanced stage. Little progress had been made with stations but it was hoped that the line would be opened in the summer.

**Extension and Amalgamation proposals**

The Leeds & Bradford Railway Act, 1844, imposed on the company obligations in addition to its main line. A connecting line from the terminus at Leeds to the North Midland Railway at Hunslet had been authorised and work was in progress. In order to combat opposition to its Bill, the Company had promised to build a line from Shipley further up the Aire Valley to Keighley. It had also undertaken to extend the line beyond Bradford and through Halifax in order to form a junction with the Manchester & Leeds Railway in the Calder Valley. In September 1844 the company decided to press ahead with the Keighley line and to extend it through Skipton to Colne where it would join the proposed East Lancashire Railway. The Act for the Shipley to Colne line received the royal assent on June 30th, 1845. A branch from Keighley to Haworth was included in the Act but not proceeded with.

A separate company, the West Yorkshire Railway, was formed to promote the Leeds & Bradford Railway's interest in the route from Bradford to Halifax and the Calder Valley. The Manchester & Leeds Railway, as its name suggests, had been planned to run to Leeds. Instead it had to be content with a terminus at Normanton

8

whence it exercised running powers over the North Midland Railway to Leeds Hunslet Lane. In the hope of gaining access to Leeds independently of the North Midland, it had joined the supporters of the Leeds and Bradford 'short line' to promote the Leeds & West Riding Junction Railway. There were thus two rival schemes to connect Bradford with the Calder Valley. The West Yorkshire scheme, backed by the Leeds & Bradford, and, therefore, indirectly by the North Midland, would have been connected to the line from Leeds to Bradford via Shipley. The Leeds & West Riding Junction Railway, backed by the Manchester & Leeds, would link the Bradford — Halifax line to the proposed 'short line' between Leeds and Bradford.

Both schemes went before Parliament in 1845 and both were rejected. The Manchester & Leeds Railway then offered an amalgamation to the Leeds & Bradford on whose behalf Hudson signified acceptance. A detailed agreement was reached in November 1845. The two railways consolidated their plans for a line from Bradford to the Calder Valley. The Manchester & Leeds would then have its independent route to Leeds by way of Halifax, Bradford and Shipley.

Meanwhile the North Midland had, on May 10th, 1844, become part of the Midland Railway. This was then the largest railway in the country and its chairman was George Hudson. The Midland must have wondered what its chairman was doing when he agreed to hand the Leeds & Bradford to the rival Manchester & Leeds Railway but the amalgamation in fact never took place. The Leeds & Bradford directors accused the Manchester & Leeds Railway of deviating from its agreement and introducing a new provision into the amalgamation Bill. This would have allowed the shares in the amalgamated company held by former Leeds & Bradford members to have become progressively diluted in value as they would have been prevented from participating in future capital projects.

On June 30th, 1846, the day the Leeds & Bradford Railway opened, Hudson offered it on a 999 year lease to the Midland Railway. The Leeds & Bradford shareholders, who of course included Hudson, would receive 10% per annum on their capital. The Midland shareholders accepted the lease on July 25th. Hudson not only spoke but voted at their meeting. This brought cries of 'you are the buyer and seller to' from critics amongst the Midland shareholders. In other words Hudson had carried out what we now call an 'insider deal'. The result was that the Leeds & Bradford Railway became part of the Midland. The terminus at Bradford was destined to remain a dead end. When the line from Bradford to Halifax was eventually built it was connected to the 'short line' between Bradford and Leeds and the gap in the railway system between Forster Square and Exchange stations continues to this day. The Leeds & Bradford Railway was vested in the

Midland by an Act of July 24th, 1851.

## Opening of the Leeds & Bradford Railway

The directors of the railway enjoyed a trip over the new line on May 30th, 1846, when a train of open wagons drawn by an engine called 'Lindsay' departed from Leeds Wellington station at 1.00 p.m. A band played in Leeds but silence greeted the train in Bradford. On the return journey, a fifteen minute stop was made at Apperley viaduct to inspect the earthworks.

A month later, following an inspection by Major-General Pasley on June 22nd, the line was formally opened on Tuesday, June 30th. This time the crowds in Bradford responded, a general holiday having been declared. Regular passenger services commenced the following day with departures from both termini every hour from 5.00 a.m. to 10.00 p.m. on weekdays, and five trains each way on Sundays. On the same day Midland trains began using the new line from Hunslet Lane to reach the more convenient Wellington station in Leeds.

Both terminal stations were incomplete at the opening date whilst very little progress had been made with the intermediate stations. At first all trains ran non stop. However temporary arrangements were quickly made to accommodate passengers at intermediate stations. Each Thursday during the first few months after the opening of the railway, 'The Bradford Observer' published the timetable. Intermediate stations first appeared as follows: Shipley July 16th; Apperley Bridge, Calverley Bridge (as it was then called) and Kirkstall, July 30th; Newlay, September 3rd. Goods traffic commenced on Monday, September 7th, 1846.

A contract was let by the board for the first permanent station on December 24th, 1846. This was at Apperley Bridge. The residents of Idle requested that a station be provided at the west end of Thackley tunnel which was the nearest point that the railway ran to their village. This station together with that at Armley made its first appearance in 'Bradshaw' in October 1847. The station at Idle was evidently not a success. It was only a temporary structure and appeared in the timetable for the last time in September 1848.

This is how 'Bradshaw' described the service during the first three months of 1847:-

## LEEDS AND BRADFORD RAILWAY
### W.E. Greenland, Secretary

From LEEDS, every hour from 6 a.m. until 9½ p.m.

On SUNDAYS, at 8½ and 9½ a.m., 2, 6 and 8½ p.m.

From BRADFORD, every hour from 6 a.m. until 9½ p.m.

On SUNDAYS, at 8½ and 9½ a.m., 2, 6 and 8½ p.m.

FARES - First Class 2s., second 1s. 6d., third 1s.

Week-day trains, except those at 10 a.m., and 2 p.m., stop at Kirkstall, Calverley Bridge, Apperley Bridge and Shipley.

The trains each way at 7, 9 and 11 a.m., 1, 3, 5, 7, and 9½ p.m. stop at Newlay Station. Sunday trains stop at all the Stations.

Trains from Bradford, at 6 a.m., and from Leeds, at 9½ p.m. are parliamentary.

In order to calculate the present day value of the fares it is necessary to multiply by approximately twenty times. This produces a fare of £2 to travel in the best carriage that the technology of the day could provide, £1.50 in the spartan second class and £1 in purgatory. The second class fare from Leeds to Bradford Exchange in 1978 was 28p. The early railways were very expensive. The main obstacle placed in the way of poorer travellers was the absence of third class carriages from many of the trains. The law only required one train per day—the 'Parliamentary'—to convey third class passengers. The Midland Railway often exceeded the legal minimum, but only from 1872 did it admit third class travellers to all its trains.

## Extension into Airedale

Work proceeded quickly following the authorisation of the extension line from Shipley. On February 13th, 1847, a locomotive was able to reach Keighley. Captain Simmons inspected the line for the Board of Trade on Saturday, March 13th, and the public opening took place on the following Tuesday, the 16th. There were eight trains each way from Bradford to Keighley on weekdays and three on Sundays. All stoppped at Shipley and Bingley. Captain Simmons returned on Saturday, August 28th, to inspect the line from Keighley to Skipton. The directors enjoyed their trial trip on September 1st and the line opened to the public on Tuesday, September 7th, 1847. Only a single line was available at first but by December double track was in use as were intermediate stations at Steeton, Kildwick and Cononley.

11

The passenger service operated from Leeds to Bradford and from Bradford to Skipton. Passengers from Leeds to Skipton changed trains at Shipley. Although there was a triangular layout at Shipley, platforms were provided only on the two sides leading to Bradford. This has always meant that trains going direct from Leeds to Skipton have either to miss stopping at Shipley or to engage in a shunting operation. The number and variety of trains travelling through from Leeds to Skipton increased as the various extensions were carried out beyond Skipton. The Midland Railway opened the Skipton - Colne line on October 2nd, 1848. The East Lancashire Railway reached Colne from Burnley on February 1st, 1849, and from April 2nd that year it became possible to run a service from Leeds to Liverpool via Skipton and Colne.

The North Western Railway, which soon became a part of the Midland, was opened from Skipton to Clapham on July 30th, 1849, and, within a year, the route to Lancaster and Morecambe was opened throughout. The line through the Aire Valley became part of the Midland route to Scotland with the opening of the Clapham to Lowgill line on October 1st, 1861. The Midland Railway's control of this route ended at Ingleton. Dissatisfaction at the handling of its traffic thence to Carlisle by the London & North Western Railway was a major factor in its determination to construct an independent route to Scotland. Passenger services over the Settle & Carlisle line finally commenced on May 1st, 1876.

**The Ilkley Branch**

On August 1st, 1865, the Midland Railway opened its line from Apperley Junction to Otley and Ilkley. The Ilkley branch falls outside the scope of this book but its trains are relevant because they augmented the service between stations on the Leeds and Bradford line. Trains from Leeds to Ilkley served stations as far as Calverley & Rodley. From Apperley Junction the branch runs alongside the main line whilst gaining height and then, within sight of Apperley Bridge station, it takes a sharp curve to the north and climbs towards Guiseley.

The only way that a service could be provided from Bradford to Ilkley was by reversal at Apperley Junction. The journey to Ilkley by this route occupied an hour. It became possible for an express train to accomplish the journey in thirty minutes when the direct line from Shipley to Guiseley was opened on December 4th, 1876. Since that date trains from Bradford have followed the Leeds line from Shipley station for about half a mile before diverging at Guiseley Junction. The opening of this line provided a diversionary route in the event of any difficulty in Thackley tunnel because a train could travel via and reverse at Guiseley. After 1888, when the branch was extended from Ilkley to Skipton, an alternative route was available in the event of an interruption to traffic at any point along the Aire Valley.

## The Floods of 1866

The option of diverting traffic via Guiseley was not yet available and Midland Railway traffic was severely disrupted when Apperley viaduct was destroyed on Friday, November 14th, 1866. West Yorkshire was badly hit and there were a number of deaths caused by the weather that day. A 'Bradford Observer' reporter travelled by the 1 p.m. train from Bradford to Otley. Instead of the 49 minutes allowed in the timetable the journey consumed three hours. The train had to make two attempts at the ascent from Apperley Junction to Guiseley. It eventually succeeded by the wrong line, the other track being blocked by an embankment slip. On the return journey the train got no further than Apperley Bridge station because the viaduct carrying the line over the river Aire had disappeared.

The Apperley Bridge station master was advised by the guard of the 4.50 p.m. Bradford to Leeds train that the viaduct appeared insecure. The station master set off on foot and was able to halt an up goods train. The driver of the train, which consisted of an engine, tender, two wagons and a guard's van, saw the station master's handlamp as he emerged from Thackley tunnel and brought the train to a stand on the viaduct. The level of the river Aire had risen considerably and was flowing through all ten arches of the viaduct instead of the usual three. According to a newspaper correspondent signing himself 'Eye witness' the train stood on the viaduct for fifteen minutes whilst the crew and the station master debated what to do. The decision was made for them when the viaduct collapsed. The engine and tender became embedded in the river whilst the van and wagons flowed downstream. Passengers who were stranded at Apperley Bridge must have faced a difficult journey home. The railway to Leeds was under three feet of water at Kirkstall whilst the road to Bradford was flooded where it crosses the river Aire below the station.

For the next week trains were terminated at Shipley and Apperley Bridge. Through passengers travelled by the Great Northern Railway from Leeds Central to Bradford Adolphus Street whence they walked to the Midland station. An editorial in the 'Bradford Observer' claimed that the Midland Railway had received just retribution for its failure to build a joint station in Bradford with the other railway companies. Various correspondents agreed and one, pursuing a similar theme, stated that the Midland Railway would have been spared the disruption to its traffic if it had built a proper route from Bradford to Ilkley.

From Saturday, November 24th, trains reverted to the normal time-table but terminated at either side of Apperley viaduct where passengers crossed a footbridge which had been built over the river, now restored to its normal width. The building of a replacement structure was commenced without delay and accomplished very quickly. Normal running was restored on January 3rd, 1867.

## Additional Stations and tracks

In 1856, a station was opened at the village of Saltaire built around Sir Titus Salt's mill near Shipley. Kirkstall Forge station, opened in 1860, took its name from the place it was built to serve. Only a few trains stopped there. Holbeck was a two level station providing interchange between the Great Northern, North Eastern and Midland Railways. The other two companies had used it since 1855 but Midland trains began to stop there in 1862. Two stations were provided on the Bradford line at Manningham, where the locomotive sheds were situated, and at Frizinghall where the opportunity was taken to replace a level crossing by a bridge at the same time. Opened on February 1st, 1875, this station was one of many in the area to have its main building situated on an overbridge from which access to the platform was by staircases.

Requests that it should provide stations between Bingley and Keighley were turned down by the Midland Railway. Crossflatts was felt to be too close to Bingley but eventually the company acknowledged the need to serve the small village of Thwaites, three quarters of a mile from Keighley. The station was opened on June 1st, 1892, and again the opportunity was taken to replace a level crossing by a bridge from which access to the platforms was gained. At first there was a weekday service of thirteen trains each way but traffic did not materialise. The number of stopping trains had dropped to four each way when closure was announced in June 1909. The 'Keighley News' accepted that the station had been a failure and could not be justified unless there was a substantial increase in the village population. Passengers to Keighley were able to use the tramway from Stockbridge as an alternative.

As traffic and services developed, some of the existing passenger stations became inadequate. The opening of the Settle & Carlisle line caused Skipton to gain importance and a new station was built to the west of the previous one. This had four platforms. Two more were added on the south side in 1888 to accommodate trains from the Ilkley line which descended into Skipton crossing over the main line with which its tracks connected beyond the station.

The decision to improve facilities at Keighley was taken in conjunction with the Great Northern Railway and the construction of a new station there with separate branch platforms is dealt with in chapter four. Kildwick moved a quarter of a mile nearer to Skipton in 1889. The next three years saw the resiting of Bingley and Steeton stations. A new and enlarged terminus came into use at Bradford on March 2nd, 1890. This station was called Market Street until 1924 when the present name of Forster Square was adopted.

14

As traffic continued to develop the capacity of the double track became strained. The busiest section was between Leeds and Shipley which, in addition to handling long distance traffic from Leeds to the north, was also part of the Midland route from the south to Bradford. With local passenger and goods traffic in addition to long distance trains the Midland Railway resolved to quadruple the track, this work being carried out in stages and completed over the years 1896 to 1910. The two pairs of tracks were designated 'fast' and 'slow' lines. Between Kirkstall and Armley the 'fast' lines crossed over the 'slow' on a flyover. Passenger trains from Leeds Wellington to Bradford Market Street usually took the 'fast' lines which were the most northerly tracks as far as the flyover. Continuing on the south side from Kirkstall to Shipley they afforded entry to the Bradford line without conflicting with trains travelling to or from Skipton. Freight trains from the south to the north found the 'slow' lines convenient. Both pairs of lines were available to passenger and goods traffic. The Ilkley trains were to be found on either side between Leeds and Apperley Junction, whilst expresses from Leeds to Skipton and beyond generally took the 'slow' lines so that they could avoid conflict with Leeds to Bradford locals.

The widening involved a new Thackley tunnel and a second Apperley viaduct. These accommodated the 'slow' lines and were opened in 1901. The tracks were realigned at various points along the route so that for some of the way the 'fast' lines were the new ones. The stations at Armley, Kirkstall, Newlay, Calverley & Rodley and Apperley Bridge were substantially rebuilt with four platforms at each. The station at Kirkstall Forge was closed when that section was widened in 1905.

Quadrupling had been carried out earlier between Shipley and Bradford, where additional goods lines were provided on the east side. Over two sections of the line north of Shipley, Bingley to Thwaites and Snaygill to Skipton, the additional goods lines were built astride the main line.

### The Bradford Through Line

Prior to 1867 Bradford had been served by three railways, each with its separate terminus. In that year the Great Northern Railway closed Adolphus Street and diverted its trains via a new connection to the Lancashire and Yorkshire station which became known as Bradford Exchange. Proposals made at that time and again in 1884 to bring all three lines into a central station met with no success. The absence of a through line was not just an inconvenience to through passengers but was a barrier helping to keep the Midland Railway out of the freight market in the industrial area to the south of Bradford. When the company obtained its West Riding Lines Act in 1898 it was prompted by a third factor which was the desire

15

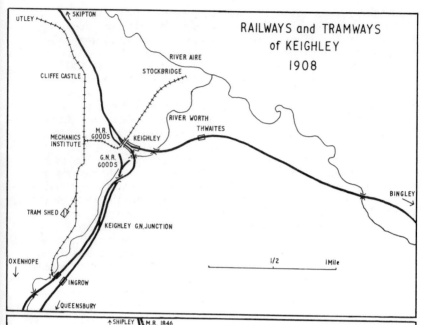

RAILWAYS and TRAMWAYS
of KEIGHLEY
1908

UTLEY

SKIPTON

RIVER AIRE

STOCKBRIDGE

CLIFFE CASTLE

RIVER WORTH
THWAITES

MECHANICS
INSTITUTE

M.R.
GOODS

KEIGHLEY

G.N.R.
GOODS

TRAM SHED

KEIGHLEY G.N.JUNCTION

OXENHOPE

BINGLEY

1/2      1 Mile

INGROW

QUEENSBURY

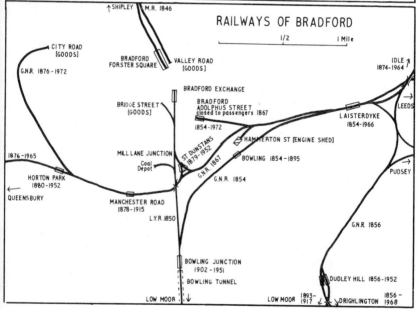

RAILWAYS OF BRADFORD

SHIPLEY   M.R. 1846

1/2      1 Mile

CITY ROAD
[GOODS]

G.N.R. 1876-1972

BRADFORD
FORSTER SQUARE

VALLEY ROAD
[GOODS]

IDLE
1874-1964

BRADFORD EXCHANGE

BRIDGE STREET
[GOODS]

BRADFORD
ADOLPHUS STREET
closed to passengers 1867

1854-1972

LEEDS

LAISTERDYKE
1854-1966

1876-1965

MILL LANE JUNCTION

Coal
Depot

ST DUNSTANS
1879-1952

HAMMERTON ST [ENGINE SHED]

BOWLING 1854-1895

G.N.R. 1867

PUDSEY

HORTON PARK
1880-1952

G.N.R. 1854

QUEENSBURY

MANCHESTER ROAD
1878-1915

L.Y.R.1850

G.N.R. 1856

BOWLING JUNCTION
1902-1951

BOWLING TUNNEL

DUDLEY HILL 1856-1952

LOW MOOR

LOW MOOR   1893-
1917

1856-
1968

DRIGHLINGTON

16

to make its main line from London to Scotland more competitive with those of its East and West Coast rivals.

The new line was to run from Royston, on the main line south of Leeds, via Thornhill and the Spen Valley to join the existing line just north of Bradford Market Street. A two mile tunnel was proposed to gain access to Bradford where the city centre would be crossed underground. The distance from Royston to Shipley would be five miles shorter than via the existing route. St. Pancras to Carlisle expresses would take the new line via Bradford and no longer serve Leeds where reversal was necessary. The main line would have connections to Dewsbury, Huddersfield and Halifax.

The Midland Railway found difficulty in raising the required capital and on three occasions, in 1901, 1904 and 1907, had to return to Parliament to seek extensions of time. Bradford Corporation sought and received assurances that the scheme would go ahead. In 1911 the project was abandoned in favour of a more modest alternative. The section from Royston to Thornhill had been built and running powers negotiated so that Midland trains could reach Huddersfield, Halifax and Bradford Exchange over the tracks of the London & North Western and the Lancashire & Yorkshire Railways. The Midland now obtained an Act for a line between Low Moor and Manningham which would cross Bradford on a viaduct and have high level platforms at Market Street station. Bradford Corporation gave support in the form of a reduction in rates. On the outbreak of the First World War work was postponed. When peace returned the Midland Railway promised that the Bradford Through Line would proceed, but the days when private capital was available for railway construction were now over and it was not built.

**Train services in 1910**

We now look at the timetable for the Leeds, Bradford and Skipton line in the year of the accession of King George V. The line had enjoyed more than sixty years of almost uninterrupted progress and the passenger train service was comprehensive. It was also complicated. The regular interval pattern of departures that was introduced on the opening of the line in 1846-47 had been very short lived and did not reappear until the diesel era. Taking the Monday to Friday service, there were eighteen departures from Leeds to Skipton. These were expresses for destinations beyond Skipton and made few stops in the Aire Valley. The majority stopped at Keighley and a number served Bingley. Some Leeds to Morecambe trains attached carriages from Bradford outside Shipley station. Passengers from Bradford and Shipley wishing to join expresses to Glasgow and Edinburgh had to change but in the reverse direction a through service was provided by a slip coach. The rear coach of the southbound express was detached and brought to a stand in Saltaire station whilst the rest of the train continued non stop to Leeds. A locomotive then hauled the slip coach to Bradford stopping, if required, to set down long distance passengers at Shipley, Frizinghall and Manningham. This arrangement, which began in 1908, ceased during the First World War.

In 1910 there were 41 trains from Leeds Wellington to Bradford Market Street. Some were expresses from south of Leeds which after reversal proceeded fast to Bradford, the majority stopping only at Shipley. Others were locals calling at most or all stations. Connections at Shipley were generally good between these trains and those on the Bradford to Skipton service. 28 trains daily from Bradford ran through to Skipton. A further twelve went as far as Keighley and two more terminated at Bingley. Between Bradford and Shipley the frequency was increased by the Ilkley branch trains. The Midland Railway operated 21 trains daily from Bradford to either Ilkley or Otley. A further nine trains ran from Bradford to Harrogate via Otley and these were worked by North Eastern Railway locomotives and rolling stock. Ten trains from Leeds left the Aire Valley for the Ilkley branch at Apperley Junction enhancing the service between the stations from Leeds to Calverley & Rodley.

The journey from Leeds to Bradford with nine stops occupied 45 minutes for the 13½ miles. The fastest express took 20 minutes. The time from Leeds to Keighley was 29 minutes for 17 miles with one stop by a through train. When the journey was by stopping trains, with a change at Shipley, it took an hour. In 1978 the fastest trains took 22 minutes but those which reversed into Shipley station required 31 minutes to reach Keighley.

Generally speaking these services enjoyed a monopoly over the available traffic. Motor transport was very much in its infancy at this time. The Leeds trams, without running in parallel with the railway, encroached within the catchment areas of stations as far as Calverley & Rodley. The Bradford trams ran to Shipley and Saltaire. In 1914 they reached Bingley but, as detailed in chapter five, they got no further. Passengers from Leeds and Bradford to Keighley could travel by the Great Northern Railway but would probably find the journey slower than by the Midland unless they had arrived at either Leeds Central or Bradford Exchange station by a connecting train as part of a longer journey.

The frequency of passenger trains was more than equalled by the goods traffic. In addition to long distance trains from south of Leeds to Bradford and to the north, there were local journeys made to the intermediate goods yards which adjoined each of the stations in the Aire Valley. At Apperley viaduct a connection was built in 1910 to the private railway system of the Bradford Corporation sewage works. This was used to carry material during construction and later to deliver coal and to despatch by-produce. A number of factories and mills along the route had private sidings.

# 2.

# The Aire Valley Line
### From the Grouping to the Present Day

## The L.M.S. period

As normality returned after the end of the First World War it became clear that the railway industry faced a radically different economic climate. By 1920 retail prices were almost three times their pre war level although they did drop during the twenties to approximately twice their pre war level by 1930. By comparison railway fares were increased by only 50%. The time honoured third class fare of 1d. per mile became 1½d. in 1918. Even if Parliament had sanctioned a greater increase, the companies would have had difficulty in enforcing it. The advent of competition on a serious scale from road transport meant that fares had to be cut. Cheap day returns became more widespread and in 1930 monthly returns were introduced at 1d. per mile.

The industry was reorganised to face the new situation. War time Government control was abolished in 1921 and permanent nationalisation ruled out in favour of a scheme for compulsory amalgamation. From 1923 the industry was dominated by four main line companies, the Midland becoming part of the London Midland & Scottish Railway whose initials 'L.M.S.' were a household name during the next 25 years.

The rationalisation of main line terminals in major cities became more urgent as a means of achieving economy and a better service to passengers and freight customers who could now look to alternative forms of transport. The L.M.S. had a stake in both Market Street and Exchange stations at Bradford but could not justify the cost of a through line despite the undisputed benefits that it would bring. In Leeds, the former Midland Railway Wellington station was situated adjacent to Leeds New station, opened in 1869 and jointly owned by the London & North Western and North Eastern Railways, now parts of the L.M.S. and L.N.E.R. respectively. A short distance away was the former Great Northern terminus at Leeds Central also part of the L.N.E.R. The two companies could not afford the necessary alterations associated with the combining of all three stations but were able to proceed with a scheme to amalgamate Leeds Wellington and Leeds New. In May 1938 these two became Leeds City.

When the Second World War started on September 3rd, 1939, the railways were again taken over by the Government. Ordinary services were curtailed but special traffic ensured that the railways were used to the utmost whilst maintenance was kept to a minimum and capital expenditure practically halted. Government control was never abandoned and on January 1st, 1948, most lines were nationalised to become British Railways.

**Nationalisation**

In deciding its policy for post war reconstruction, British Railways pinned its faith in the continued development of the steam locomotive. So with new locomotive classes replacing many of the old worn out engines the pattern of train services continued with only a very slow move towards restoration of pre-war standards of service. In 1957 there were 17 departures from Keighley to Bradford Forster Square on Mondays to Fridays which was about half the number there had been in 1938. Most of these trains gave a connection at Shipley for Leeds. The number of through trains to Leeds at 13 was about the same as in 1938. These were the through trains from the Morecambe and Carlisle lines.

In 1955 there was a strike by the majority of drivers and firemen which lasted 17 days spanning the Whitsuntide holiday. Only a skeleton service ran between Leeds, Bradford, Keighley and Skipton. Afterwards the 'Keighley News' commented that, whilst there had been serious disruption to normal life in other parts particularly in London, the effect of the strike had been minimal in Keighley. It went on to add that the railways were obviously no longer as vital as had previously been supposed.

A major reinvestment was needed if the railways were to face up to road competition. Such a scheme for the modernisation of British Railways was announced in 1955. Amongst far reaching proposals were the replacement of steam power by diesel on non electrified lines and the fitting of continuous brakes on all freight trains thereby ending what the B.R. chairman described as 'Emmet-like trains going clanketty-clank through our countryside'. Steam power was eliminated in 1968 but unfitted freight trains are still to be seen. It was in the field of local passenger services that the first effects of the modernisation plan were seen. During the period 1954 to 1961 British Railways introduced a large number of diesel multiple units into service in place of local steam trains.

On January 5th, 1959, the local services in the Aire Valley were completely handed over to diesel operation. There was a basic hourly interval service from Leeds to Bradford, Bradford to Skipton via Keighley, Leeds to Ilkley and Bradford to Ilkley. Steam power remained on the longer distance trains for some years until diesel locomotives gradually took over in the mid-sixties. 'Bradshaw' for 1960 shows the effect of dieselisation on the service. Again taking Monday to Friday departures from Keighley, there were 24 trains to Bradford Forster Square and 14 through to Leeds which could also be reached by most of the Bradford trains changing at Shipley. There were 30 trains per day from Bradford Forster Square to Leeds City. Two thirds of these were diesel multiple units stopping at most stations, giving an hourly interval service with peak hour extras. The others were steam trains stopping only at Shipley and bound for destinations south of Leeds.

A criticism levelled at the modernisation plan was that it did little but change the motive power. The local stations continued to be fully staffed and, in order to economise, some of them were closed at quiet times so that the new diesel trains ran through without stopping. This applied in the evenings and on Sundays. By 1963 the only intermediate stations with a Sunday service were Shipley, Bingley, Keighley Kildwick and Cononley. Kirkstall and Saltaire were open on Sundays for three months in the summer. The Ilkley trains ran on Sundays during this same three month period only. Publicity for the improved services was poor. The attractive timetable leaflets of today were only just beginning whilst the idea of providing free car parking at stations was unheard of at that time. Nevertheless the public reaction to the diesel trains on this and on most other lines was favourable. A table showing the increases in patronage following the early dieselisation schemes in the North Eastern Region appears in 'Trains Illustrated' for January 1959, Leeds Central to Bradford Exchange featuring as the most successful of the early schemes.

**The closures**

From the mid fifties onwards British Railways began to incur a trading loss. At first it was hoped that the modernisation plan coupled with the elimination of some of the least used lines would restore profitability. This did not happen but the Government was still determined that the railways should be financially self supporting and in 1963 it accepted the Beeching Report. This recommended that the desired goal would be achieved at the cost of closing more than half the system. Previously a closure had to be approved by a Transport Users Consultative Committee but under the Transport Act 1962 the powers of these bodies were reduced and the final decision left with the Minister of Transport. Users of a passenger service were allowed to object on the grounds of personal hardship but were not allowed to question the grounds for closure. One or two closures were refused especially in the months prior to the 1964 general election. One such was the Settle &

Carlisle local service which was closed on a subsequent application. The closures of the fifties and early sixties, some of which had been fiercely opposed like that of the Worth Valley branch (see next chapter), seemed trivial by comparison with what was now to follow. The revised closure machinery ensured that most cases that might have been rejected previously would now be nodded through.

The Beeching Report recommended the withdrawal of local services in the Aire Valley and the closure to passenger traffic of the Shipley to Bradford Forster Square line. The complete closure of the Ilkley branch, the Settle & Carlisle line, the alternative route via Ingleton and the Midland route to Morecambe via Lancaster was also planned. It was proposed that a passenger service would continue to operate from Leeds to Morecambe via Carnforth. Shipley, Bingley, Keighley and Skipton stations would be the only ones to remain open in the Aire Valley. On May 27th and 28th, 1964, the Transport Users Consultative Committee met in Ilkley to consider objections to the closure of 22 stations in Airedale and Wharfedale. At stake were local trains between Leeds and Bradford Forster Square, Bradford and Skipton via Keighley and all services to Ilkley.

It was claimed that there were only 17 passengers regularly using Calverley & Rodley station which was remote from both Calverley and Rodley. At Apperley Bridge the principal traffic came from Woodhouse Grove School which adjoins the station. This is a boarding school and might have generated greater traffic had the station survived to see the introduction of student rail cards and greater mobility amongst young people. School traffic was also prominent at Frizinghall. The author was amongst the passengers alighting there to attend Bradford Grammar School at that time. Users of Cononley station drew attention to the remoteness of their village from the main road and bus route between Keighley and Skipton. British Railways claimed that through Leeds to Bradford passengers would be accommodated by the 'short line' to Bradford Exchange. Armley Moor station on that line was offered as an alternative for the time being to Armley Canal Road but it was also proposed to close that station at a later date. The greatest opposition to the closure proposals was organised by the commuters from Ilkley. In September 1964 the Minister of Transport announced that he would defer any decision on their case. For the time being trains would continue to run from Leeds and Bradford to Ilkley but they would stop only at the stations on the branch and at Shipley. Subject to providing extra buses at Cononley the remainder of the closures were accepted. Armley Canal Road, Kirkstall, Newlay, Calverley & Rodley, Apperley Bridge, Frizinghall, Manningham, Saltaire and Steeton stations closed on March 20th, 1965. Kildwick and Cononley survived one

23

more day because they still enjoyed a year round Sunday service.

The reduced services came into effect on Monday, March 22nd, 1965. The number of through trains between Leeds and Skipton was increased and most became diesel multiple unit workings. Stops at Shipley were introduced, the trains having to stop in the station twice and to reverse at Bradford Junction. Bradford Forster Square to Skipton trains were reduced in number and terminated at Keighley. The Ilkley trains remained virtually unchanged in frequency. Through trains to and from St. Pancras, the Midlands and south-west continued to make their way after reversal at Leeds City to Shipley and Bradford Forster Square.

In 1959 a scheme had been announced for the rebuilding of Leeds City station and a new track layout which would enable Leeds Central to be closed. Work on the project was halted in 1962. When it resumed the plans had been revised in the expectation that the withdrawal of many of the services would permit a simpler layout. Because some of the closures then envisaged have not taken place the present layout suffers capacity problems. The new arrangements came into use on May 1st, 1967. The former Leeds New station became the passenger terminus and Wellington the parcels depot for all trains into Leeds. From the same date, the remaining through trains between Leeds and Bradford Forster Square were withdrawn. At the latter terminus two of the six platforms were left to handle the remaining trains to Ilkley and Keighley, the rest being used exclusively for parcels. All passengers between Leeds and Bradford must now use the line to Bradford Exchange. The 'fast' lines between Leeds and Thackley Junction were then taken out of use. The track was also reduced to double between Shipley and Manningham where in order to release the station site for sale, the tracks were slewed so as to give faster running into the Bradford goods depot. The passenger trains, which it was then envisaged would be withdrawn, have to slow down to 20 miles per hour. The four track sections were also reduced at Bingley and Skipton. The closure of the intermediate goods depots took place during the middle and late sixties. Only Shipley and Keighley depots remain open as public delivery sidings. The private sidings at Kirkstall Forge and the connection to Esholt Sewage Works have also been closed.

In 1967 the Government announced plans for a less truncated railway system than had been envisaged by Beeching. Threat of closure was lifted from some lines but the Leeds - Skipton - Morecambe line was added to the list of passenger closures. It was intended that freight traffic would continue and that Skipton would retain a passenger service, but only via Colne. Ironically, the Skipton - Colne line was closed to all traffic in 1970 but closure of the Leeds - Morecambe line has not been seriously threatened. The Settle & Carlisle line also survives.

**Midland Railway 4-4-0 No. 458 near Utley with an Edinburgh - St. Pancras express. (Jack Blades).**

**Ex-Midland Railway 2-4-0 No. 242 near Bingley with a Leeds - Carnforth train in 1932. (W. Hubert Foster).**

Ex-Midland Railway 4-4-0 No. 409 pauses at Keighley with a Skipton - Bradford (Forster Square) local train in August 1947. (W.A. Camwell).

'Royal Scot' class 4-6-0 No. 46103 hurries through Keighley with the down 'Thames-Clyde Express' in February 1955. (John Oxley).

Calverley & Rodley station in May 1957, with 'Compound' 4-4-0 No. 41071 on the 'fast' lines and a two-coach local on the 'slow' lines. (J.C.W. Halliday).

Newlay station in 1905, shortly after quadrupling of this section of the main line had taken place. (Locomotive & General Railway Photographs).

'Compound' No. 41191 halts at Skipton with a Morecambe - Leeds train in June 1958. (J.C.W. Halliday).

5MT 4-6-0 No. 44904 heads a northbound train out of Skipton in June 1964. The Ilkley-line platforms are just visible on the extreme right. (Peter E. Baughan).

Saltaire station, about 1900. The station was opened in 1856 to serve Titus Salt's 'Palace of Industry'. (collection of David Joy).

Exterior of Bradford (Forster Square) station in 1924 with tramcars still very much in evidence. (collection of David Joy).

A Bradford (Forster Square) - Keighley diesel unit leaves Shipley in June 1975. The main line curve is on the left. (Stuart Baker).

A diesel unit in white livery approaches Shipley on a Bradford (Forster Square) - Ilkley working in March 1977. (Martin Bairstow).

Class 47 No. 47053 at speed near Crossflatts in April 1976 with a Nottingham - Glasgow express. (Martin Bairstow).

A coal train in charge of No. D532 approaches Thackley tunnel in July 1972. The track bed of the former 'fast' lines can be seen on the right. (Stuart Baker).

**3F 0-6-0 No. 43586, the engine which worked the last train to Oxenhope, outside Keighley shed. (M.H. Davison).**

**The signalman at Keighley GN Junction waits for the single line token from a train approaching from Oxenhope, February 1955. (John Oxley).**

In 1968 the Minister of Transport announced that he did not intend to give the decision on the Ilkley line that had been deferred four years previously. He invited British Railways to put forward a fresh closure case and this was linked to a proposal to close Bradford Forster Square to passenger traffic. The T.U.C.C. heard objections in May 1969 but more than three years elapsed before there was any further development. In August 1972 the Government announced a reprieve for the Leeds - Ilkley service, approval for the withdrawal of Bradford - Keighley trains and a plan to run trains from Bradford to Ilkley by the pre-1876 route involving reversal at Apperley Junction.

Local government reorganisation was eighteen months away but it was known that railway transport was going to become the concern of the new West Yorkshire County Council. Bradford Corporation stepped in with a subsidy to keep the services as they were and requested that the smaller councils in the proposed Bradford Metropolitan District should participate. Denholme Urban District Council, not having seen a passenger train since 1955, understandably refused. Baildon took the opportunity to negotiate the reopening of its station on the Ilkley branch, which, though closed in 1953, was still substantially intact. It was hoped that others might follow, particularly Frizinghall. This station, closed on March 20th, 1965, was demolished in March 1972. The county council having negotiated its reopening in 1974 declined to pay the cost of reinstating the platforms. The Bradford Corporation intervention, which was without precedent anywhere else, bought time and prevented a move which might have been difficult to reverse later.

**The present day**

If the financial considerations which led to the Beeching Report were adopted now the entire railway system would be closed. The notion that the railway network could be systematically pruned until only the profitable lines remained has been likened by the present chairman of British Railways to peeling an onion in the hope of reaching the core. The West Yorkshire County Council has recently assumed financial responsibility for the passenger services in the county. It was decided to support the retention of almost all the remaining lines despite the subsidies required. It accepts that the cost of increased road congestion together with the residual railway costs, which are not all immediately extinguished on closure, outweighs the cost of subsidy. The hope that more than a minority of displaced rail passengers would transfer to buses is not held. The majority of passengers own cars and use the trains as a preferable way of getting into Leeds and Bradford or as a feeder service to 'inter city' trains. The volume of passenger traffic is buoyant at present.

The West Yorkshire County Council appears to have accepted that the railways are an expensive commitment and, unless it is going to dispense with them altogether, it is going to make the best use of them. Hopes of improvements are entertained. Work is in progress at Shipley on the construction of a fifth platform for Leeds - Skipton trains on the inside of the triangle. It is intended that, at a later date, an alteration in the track layout will allow trains in the opposite direction to use the same platform instead of having to shunt into and out of the present station.

In the 1978 timetable there are twenty trains on weekdays from Leeds to Skipton and one which terminates at Keighley. Three of these are through trains from Nottingham to Carlisle or Glasgow. These are locomotive hauled and do not stop at Shipley or Bingley. The remainder are diesel multiple units, some of which continue to Morecambe. There are eleven trains from Bradford Forster Square to Keighley. Passengers from Bradford to Keighley and beyond can sometimes use an Ilkley train and change at Shipley. The frequency of freight trains is only a fraction of what it once was. An important traffic in limestone of up to three thirty-wagon trains per day runs through the Aire Valley from the quarry at Rylstone, near Grassington, to Leeds, Hull or Teesside. Most parcels traffic to and from Bradford is handled at Forster Square station, a large proportion of this being derived from one mail order company.

A feature of the inter war period was the range of cheap excursions to the coast. This class of traffic fell prey to the family car but, in recent years, there has been a growth in longer distance excursions. At Keighley this is a two way traffic for, whilst passengers depart for destinations in Scotland or on the south coast, incoming excursionists change trains there for Haworth. These special trains usually operate on Saturdays outside the peak summer period.

**A description of the route**

Most trains from Leeds to Skipton depart from platform two at Leeds. This is in the reconstructed station which stands on the site of the former Leeds New. To the right are the platforms used by parcel trains in the former Midland Railway Wellington station. The lines from both the New and Wellington stations converge into four tracks over the Leeds & Liverpool Canal bridge. The first line to diverge is that used by expresses to London via Doncaster, and then comes the triangular junction with the Midland main line to Sheffield. No regular passenger service has been carried on the spur avoiding Leeds since the turn of the century. Immediately beyond is Whitehall Junction where the lines to Huddersfield and Bradford Exchange leave to tackle the difficult gradient on the left. The layout here was altered in 1967 in order to give

Bradford Exchange trains access to the Midland line at this point. Previously the Great Northern Railway crossed over the Midland and terminated at Leeds Central, the two level Holbeck station allowing interchange for passengers.

Beyond Holbeck the four track line used to gain two more tracks which carried North Eastern Railway trains out of Leeds Central. These continued to run in parallel as far as the present Wortley Junction where the North Eastern Railway Harrogate line diverges to the right. At the present time, the track is quadruple from Leeds to this junction where it becomes double, but prior to 1967 four tracks continued to Shipley. The pair remaining in use are the former 'slow' lines and are on the south side of the formation as far as the site of the Kirkstall flyover. Armley Canal Road station was in a cutting and had two long island platforms. At its closure in 1965 it was the only station between Leeds and Skipton with electric lights apart from Keighley, the others being still illuminated by gas.

Loops are retained at Kirkstall so that goods trains can be overtaken. The station here had two side platforms and a central island, a pattern which also prevailed at the next three stations. The ruins of Kirkstall Abbey can be seen on the right of the line which curves gently to the left. At Kirkstall Forge, the sidings have now been removed. Beyond Newlay the line passes through a deep rock cutting to reach the next station at Calverley & Rodley where there were sidings on both sides of the line, used for stabling surplus carriages and brake vans, until they were removed in the late sixties. The distance from Calverley to the station was a mile and a half, part of the route being by a footpath. The village of Rodley was a little closer but only a few houses were situated within easy reach.

At Apperley Junction the Ilkley line diverges to the right and begins its 1 in 60 ascent running alongside the main line before bearing off into wooded country on the climb to Guiseley. Apperley Bridge goods yard occupied the angle between the branch and the main line. On the left is Woodhouse Grove School which provided much traffic for the station whose platforms were reached by staircases from the main building which was situated on the road bridge above. The two principal earthworks are passed in the next section. Because the line was widened at the turn of the century, these appear in duplicate with the redundant Apperley viaduct and Thackley tunnel on the left of the structures still in use.

Thackley Junction lies near the site of the short lived Idle station and four tracks are retained over the next mile which runs alongside the canal. At Shipley, Guiseley Junction, the line from Ilkley to Bradford joins on the right. Immediately opposite there was a Great Northern signalbox called Shipley Junction which controlled, from the G.N. side, the connection between that company's Bradford - Idle - Shipley branch and the Midland Railway. Great

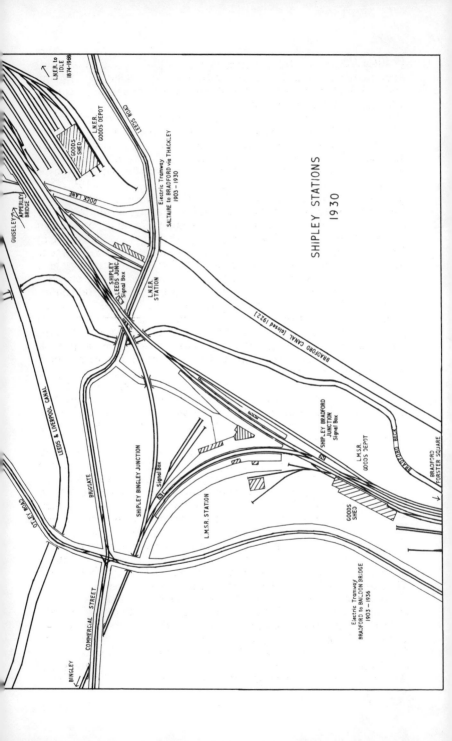

SHIPLEY STATIONS
1930

Northern passenger trains did not use this connection but ran into their own single platform terminus, the remains of which can still be seen on the left.

As the Bradford line runs into platforms three and four at Shipley, the main line bears sharply to the right. Work is in progress in building a platform on this curve. The third side of the triangle, which carries platforms one and two, joins at Shipley, Bingley Junction. The main line continues along the valley of the river Aire soon passing the village of Saltaire. Bingley station is approached through a 151 yard tunnel; here the site of the former goods yard is derelict even though the passenger station remains open. Three Rise and, beyond that, Five Rise Locks can be seen on the canal. The wide earthworks confirm that the section from here to Thwaites used to be quadruple track.

Keighley station has recently undergone a facelift which took several years to complete and which has left it looking rather bare without any shelter over the platforms. The goods yard remains open for traffic but the sidings have been rationalised. All traces of the small engine shed have gone. The three stations between Keighley and Skipton were all at level crossings and were closed in 1965. Speculation about their reopening is heard but, ironically, the one where the platforms are still in place, Cononley, is outside the boundary of the West Yorkshire County Council from whom any initiative on reopening will come.

Although the Skipton-Ilkley line is closed the bridge across the main line on the approach to Skipton still carries rail traffic thanks to the quarry trains from Rylstone, now the terminus of the Grassington branch. A bitumen terminal occupies the site of the original Skipton station. Four platforms remain in use at the present station, the main buildings leading on to the up (Leeds bound) platform two. Platform one is a bay for trains starting for Leeds while platforms three and four are an island for traffic in the northbound direction. Before closure of the Colne line in 1970, platform four was used for trains to and from East Lancashire. Platforms five and six are separate, disused and situated on a rising gradient for the former Ilkley and Grassington trains.

### The Bradford line and signalling

The present appearance of the branch from Shipley to Bradford gives little clue to its former main line status. The track is now double from Shipley, Bradford Junction as far as Manningham Junction. The goods yard at Shipley is on the right and deals with incoming coal and outgoing scrap metal. The former goods lines on the left of the passenger lines are removed as are all remains of the stations at Frizinghall and Manningham. Gone too are the engine sheds and carriage sidings which occupied the area to the left of Manningham station.

Beyond the road bridge at Manningham the passenger and goods lines separate. The former now bear to the right, negotiating 20 miles per hour crossovers to reach Forster Square station, while the goods lines run in parallel to Valley Road depot. The track layout, though considerably rationalised, is still extensive. The station has three island platforms but, since 1967, only platforms one and two, on the west side, have served the local passenger trains while the other four platforms have dealt with the large parcels traffic.

The reduction in traffic, helped to some extent by the elimination of the slowest trains, has allowed the closure of many of the intermediate signalboxes. Since 1967 Leeds power box has controlled the line as far as Armley. From there to both Skipton and Bradford mechanical signalling is still employed, though with fewer boxes than previously and with some of the semaphore signals replaced by colour lights.Signal boxes remain in use at Kirkstall Junction; Apperley Junction; Thackley Junction; Shipley, Guiseley Junction; Shipley, Bingley Junction; Bingley; Keighley; Steeton; Kildwick; Cononley; Skipton South; and Skipton North. Boxes on the Bradford line are at Shipley, Bradford Junction; Manningham Junction; and Bradford Forster Square. Most of these will disappear when the Leeds signalbox area is extended northwards.

# 3. The Keighley & Worth Valley Railway

### Proposals to build a branch line

Three and a half miles to the south of Keighley lies the village of Haworth, well known for its association with the Brontë family. Members of the family invested in early railways whilst Branwell Brontë was for a short time employed by the Manchester & Leeds Railway. Although none of them lived long enough to see the construction of a line to Haworth, the Brontë sisters have, for over a century, posthumously helped to sustain the level of passenger traffic on the Worth Valley Railway by attracting tourists to the area.

When Charlotte and Anne Brontë visited their publisher in London in 1848 they set out from Haworth on foot and endured a thunderstorm before reaching Keighley station. They may have wished that one of the two recent abortive schemes to connect Haworth to Keighley by rail had met with more success. One of the extensions authorised by the Leeds & Bradford Railway Act, 1845, was for a branch to Haworth but it was not proceeded with. During the same year the Manchester, Hebden Bridge & Keighley Junction Railway invited the public to subscribe £350,000 for the construction of a line from Hebden Bridge through Haworth to Keighley. This line would have been about twelve miles in length and would have passed under Oxenhope Moor through a long tunnel. Hebden Bridge, in the Calder Valley, was already served by the Manchester & Leeds Railway. The proposed line would have linked this with the Aire Valley extension of the Leeds & Bradford Railway which, as described in chapter one, had recently been authorised. This was the period of the 'Railway Mania'. The necessary capital was not forthcoming and the scheme failed to make any progress.

In October 1861 a deputation of local business interests waited upon the Midland Railway company in Derby and proposed a line from Keighley through Haworth to Oxenhope. In seeking the support of the Midland Railway for their application to Parliament they drew attention to the number of mills that lay along the route. Agreement was reached that a local company would be formed to raise capital and build the line and that, upon completion, it would be operated by the Midland Railway. The traffic receipts would be split equally between the two companies.

By the Keighley & Worth Valley Railway Act, 1862, the company was incorporated and authorised to purchase the land required to build the line. The track was to be single commencing at a junction near Keighley station on the Midland Railway, the route to Oxenhope being just under five miles in length. Sufficient land was acquired and the bridges made wide enough to accommodate double track should it ever be required at a future date. For most of its independent existence the chairman of the Keighley & Worth Valley Railway company was Mr Isaac Holden, a prominent local businessman who became a Member of Parliament in 1865. He was the first Member to sit for Keighley when it became a constituency in 1885.

On January 19th, 1864, the directors awarded the contract for building the line to John Metcalfe of Bradford, the first sod being ceremonially cut on February 9th by Isaac Holden. A problem was encountered during the construction of the 150 yard tunnel at Ingrow. Situated above was the Wesley Place Methodist Church which was a new building, the foundation stone having been laid by Isaac Holden on March 10th, 1863. The church was hit by subsidence and had to be taken down and rebuilt on an adjacent site where it survived until the 1950s, the present structure being the original Sunday school building. The trustees took their case to arbitration and recovered £1,980 from the railway company.

By the autumn of 1866 the new railway was almost ready for use. The contractor was able to run a train to Oxenhope and back on November 1st but hopes of an early opening received a setback from the floods which hit West Yorkshire on November 14th. Damage was sustained in a number of places including Haworth station and Damems where 40 yards of embankment were washed away leaving the track suspended.

**The opening of the branch**

Outstanding work was completed and the opening date fixed for Saturday, April 13th, 1867. The first train, conveying invited guests, consisted of a tank engine, seven coaches and a guards van. The weather being bad, the rails were wet and the train slipped to a halt on the 1 in 58 gradient outside Keighley. It set back to start again and this time it was successful in getting clear of Keighley but stopped between Oakworth and Haworth and had to complete the journey in two sections. Whilst the guests repaired to the Mechanics Institute, Haworth, for the celebration dinner, members of the public made their first train journeys through the Worth Valley.

The following Monday saw the introduction of a regular passenger service with six trains each way on weekdays and two on

Sundays. The following is the service which appeared in 'Bradshaw' for October 1867. By that time the tiny station at Damems had been brought into use:

| | WEEKDAYS | | | | | S.O. | SUNDAYS | | | |
|---|---|---|---|---|---|---|---|---|---|---|
| | A.M. | P.M. | P.M. | P.M. | P.M. | P.M. | A.M. | A.M. | P.M. | P.M. |
| Keighley | 8.35 | 12.20 | 2.20 | 5.00 | 6.40 | 8.30 | 7.50 | 10.40 | 2.05 | 7.20 |
| Ingrow | 8.41 | 12.26 | 2.26 | 5.06 | 6.45 | 8.36 | 7.56 | 10.46 | 2.11 | 7.26 |
| Damems | 8.44 | - | - | - | 6.48 | - | - | - | - | - |
| Oakworth | 8.47 | 12.32 | 2.32 | 5.12 | 6.50 | 8.42 | 8.02 | 10.52 | 2.17 | 7.32 |
| Haworth | 8.53 | 12.38 | 2.38 | 5.18 | 6.54 | 8.48 | 8.08 | 10.58 | 2.23 | 7.38 |
| Oxenhope | 9.00 | 12.45 | 2.45 | 5.25 | 7.00 | 8.55 | 8.15 | 11.05 | 2.30 | 7.45 |

| | WEEKDAYS | | | | | | SUNDAYS | | | |
|---|---|---|---|---|---|---|---|---|---|---|
| | A.M. | A.M. | P.M. | P.M. | P.M. | P.M | A.M. | P.M. | P.M. | P.M. |
| Oxenhope | 8.00 | 9.20 | 1.30 | 3.50 | 5.50 | 7.10 | 8.30 | 12.55 | 6.30 | 8.00 |
| Haworth | 8.06 | 9.26 | 1.36 | 3.56 | 5.56 | 7.14 | 8.36 | 1.0! | 6.36 | 8.06 |
| Oakworth | 8.12 | 9.32 | 1.42 | 4.02 | 6.02 | 7.18 | 8.42 | 1.07 | 6.42 | 8.12 |
| Damems | 8.15 | - | - | - | 6.05 | - | - | - | - | - |
| Ingrow | 8.18 | 9.38 | 1.48 | 4.08 | 6.08 | 7.23 | 8.48 | 1.13 | 6.48 | 8.18 |
| Keighley | 8.25 | 9.45 | 1.55 | 4.15 | 6.15 | 7.30 | 8.55 | 1.20 | 6.55 | 8.25 |

S.O. - SATURDAYS ONLY

The following appears in the 'Keighley News' for May 25th, six weeks after the opening:

"Since the Worth Valley Railway was opened it has been the means already of bringing thousands of visitors to the ancient village of Haworth. During the past few Sundays, hundreds have been seen enjoying the pure air and mountain breezes in the romantic neighbourhood. To all appearances it is very likely to become a general pleasure locality in the summer months."

Goods traffic was handled from July 1st, 1867. The contractor remained responsible for maintaining the branch for twelve months before handing over to the Midland Railway in April 1868. The revenue continued to be shared with the local company until the Midland purchased the line on July 1st, 1881.

The local company seems to have had problems with the Midland Railway throughout this period. The balance sheet at June 30th, 1881, showed an amount due by the Midland Railway of £9,942 7s 5d. composed of sundry items in dispute between the companies. At an extraordinary general meeting held on August 22nd, 1885, it was admitted that the line, 'whilst being an immense advantage to the Worth Valley had not been very profitable for individual shareholders.' The K.W.V.R. company derived no financial recompense for the benefit accruing to the Midland Railway from the additional main line traffic brought about by goods and passengers travelling to and from the branch line. The

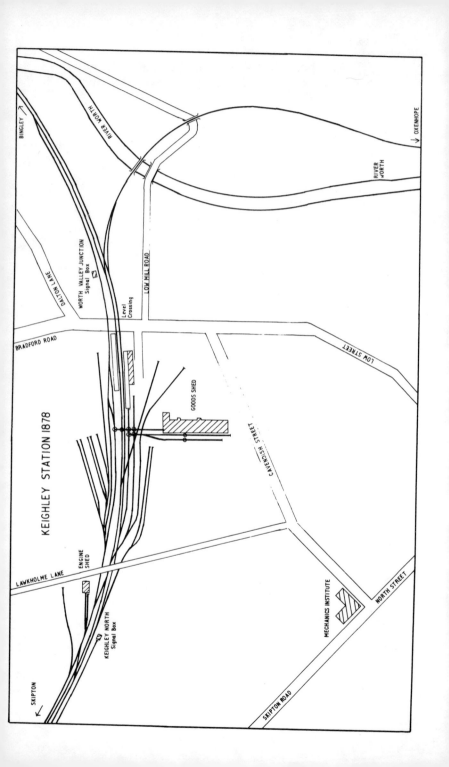

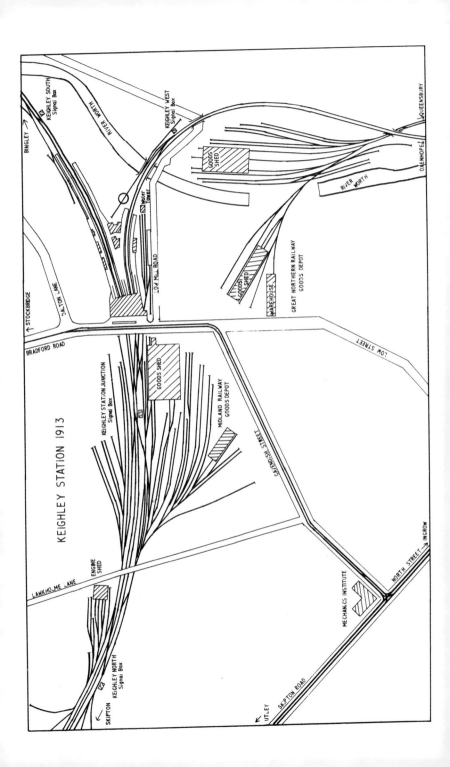

KEIGHLEY STATION 1913

Worth Valley Railway was a great deal more successful than would appear from the rather disappointing dividends paid to its shareholders. The Midland take over coincides with the agreement to allow the Great Northern Railway access into Keighley and we can conclude that the main line company was so powerful in relation to the local line that it could settle its accounts as and when it pleased and could take complete control when it became convenient to use the line in negotiations with another main line railway. The Keighley and Worth Valley Company remained in existence as ground landlords receiving an annual rent until it was dissolved under the Midland Railway Act, 1886.

## Development of services and improvements to the branch line

In 1880 the number of passenger trains had increased to nine on weekdays and five on Sundays. By the turn of the century there were fifteen weekday passenger trains. This and the corresponding increase in freight traffic necessitated an increase in the capacity of the line. The opening of the Great Northern Railway to Keighley, described in the next chapter, brought a new station at Keighley in 1883 and double track for three quarters of a mile thence to Keighley G.N. Junction. Between Oakworth and Haworth the line crossed the Vale Mill dam on a wooden viaduct, 1,033 feet long with thirty spans. After 25 years of use, major repairs to the structure were necessary and the Midland Railway decided to build a new alignment avoiding the dam. Opened on November 6th, 1892, the new route involved a high embankment, five under-bridges and the 75 yard Mytholmes tunnel. Passing loops for goods trains only were built at Oakworth and Haworth and electric token working introduced to control the single line on April 4th, 1900.

The number of bookings from Haworth to certain destinations on Whit Tuesday 1909 was recorded in the 'Keighley News'. This gives a clue to the pattern of journeys made by passengers originating at a branch line station. The numbers are in addition to local bookings and journeys by visitors to Haworth:

| | | | | |
|---|---|---|---|---|
| Morecambe | day 54 | half day 61 | Appleby | 30 |
| Grassington | day 14 | half day 15 | Aysgarth | 14 |
| Bradford | day 8 | half day 46 | Hawes | 13 |
| Liverpool | 10 | | Leeds | 5 |
| Ingleton | 6 | | Ambleside | 3 |

During the L.M.S. period push-pull working was introduced so that the train could be driven, in the Oxenhope to Keighley direction, from the leading coach with the engine remaining at the rear. This arrangement cut down the turn round time at Keighley and Oxenhope which on a short branch line was disproportionate to the journey time.

## Drift towards closure

Cuts in service followed the outbreak of the Second World War, and when peace returned these were only partially restored. On the Aire Valley line, the Ilkley branch and most other lines in West Yorkshire, the passenger services remained well below the pre-war level until the advent of the diesel multiple unit. 'Bradshaw' for 1957 shows ten trains from Keighley to Oxenhope on Mondays to Fridays as against 17 in 1938. The timetable was geared to serve early morning work people as the departure times from Keighley clearly show:

6.00 a.m.; 6.50;    7.49;    1.15 p.m.; 4.05;    4.47;
5.37;      6.27;    7.34 (Except Fridays):      9.10

The Saturday service was better but there had been no trains at all on Sundays for some years. This was at a time when car ownership was expanding rapidly.

The number of goods trains had also declined and it was possible to operate the branch without the intermediate passing loops. Oakworth and Haworth signal boxes were closed in 1956 and the line from Keighley G.N. Junction to Oxenhope worked as one single line section. Damems station was closed on May 21st, 1949; it had been little used.

Threat of closure descended upon the Worth Valley line during April 1959. British Railways put their case for closure to the Transport Users Consultative Committee and at a public hearing, held on September 1st, 1959, users of the service voiced their objections. B.R. claimed that continued operation of the loss making service conflicted with their statutory duty to seek financial self sufficiency. The local passengers claimed that the line was well used despite the poor service and that an improvement similar to that which had recently taken place on the Bradford—Skipton line was justified. The committee declined to make a decision at that stage.

The Mayor of Keighley, Councillor H. Hammond, called a public meeting for September 21st and pressed the case for retention of the railway at subsequent meetings with B.R. and the T.U.C.C. These efforts to resist closure met with initial success. On June 13, 1960, an improved service was introduced with fifteen trains each way Mondays to Fridays and twenty on Saturdays, the push-pull steam train having given way to a diesel multiple unit. B.R. claimed that the increase in patronage was not sufficient to alter their case for closure. In February 1961, the members of the T.U.C.C. travelled over the line and subsequently consented to closure. The passenger service was to be withdrawn at the end of the year and goods facilities in the following June.

The last passenger train was the 11.15 p.m. from Keighley on Saturday, December 30th, 1961. It was a four coach diesel multiple unit and worked a return service instead of coming back empty as was provided for in the timetable. About 150 passengers travelled on the last train.

## The Preservation Society

Some of the supporters of the line were far from happy about this turn of events especially as the diesel service had been given such a short trial. During 1961, as closure began to look more certain, the idea was floated that the line could be run by a voluntary society. After a preliminary meeting had been held in January 1962, a public meeting was called for Thursday, March 1st, at the Temperance Hall, Keighley to form the Keighley & Worth Valley Railway Preservation Society. The chairman was Mr. G.R. Cryer who, following in the steps of Isaac Holden, subsequently became Member of Parliament for Keighley.

The notion of a voluntary society operating a railway was not new, the narrow gauge Talyllyn Railway having been operated in this way since 1951. More recently the Bluebell Railway Preservation Society had taken a lease over the former B.R. line from Horsted Keynes to Sheffield Park in Sussex. It was hoped that the Keighley to Oxenhope line could be leased from B.R. and services resumed at an early date. On June 23rd, 1962, the society chartered a special train from Bradford Forster Square to Oxenhope and back. It was hauled by locomotive No. 43586 which had been a familiar engine on the Worth Valley freight trains. Goods traffic having ceased the previous weekend this was the last train operated by British Railways on the line.

The proposal that the line should be leased was rejected by B.R. who insisted on outright sale. The society saw little hope of raising the required capital but, in September 1964, was able to announce that an arrangement had been negotiated whereby reopening could be achieved. The society was to promote a limited company which would buy the railway from B.R. for £45,000, the purchase price together with interest being payable in equal instalments over 25 years. An obstacle was removed in June 1965 with the withdrawal of the remaining goods trains from Keighley to Ingrow (Great Northern). It had been envisaged that B.R. would retain one track from Keighley station to G.N. Junction and lease the other to the new company. The section to be sold was now extended to the entrance to Keighley station where platform four was to be leased. The new company, called Keighley & Worth Valley Light Railway Limited, was incorporated on February 8th, 1966. A majority of the shares were allotted to nominees of the preservation society who exercise full control over the company.

The next step was for B.R. to apply for the branch line to become a light railway under the Light Railways Act, 1896. This piece of legislation was designed to reduce the cost of constructing new railways in rural areas but has been used in recent years by preservation schemes because it provides the only way of transferring ownership of a railway without a special Act of Parliament. Optimistic reports that reopening would take place in 1965 or 1966 were dashed. In October 1967 the British Railways (Keighley & Worth Valley) Light Railway Order was made. The next step was for an order transferring the powers and obligations from British Railways to the new company but two objections threatened to delay this. The bus company was placated with an agreement not to undercut bus fares for a period of seven years. Keighley Corporation believed that the new company would be unable to meet its responsibilities for maintaining bridges and withdrew its objection only after an agreement had been signed giving it a preferential claim over certain of the railway's assets in the event of the project failing.

**Reopening**

Following inspection by Col. J.R.H. Robertson on June 8th, the reopening date was fixed for Saturday, June 29th, 1968. A six coach train left Keighley at 2.35 p.m. hauled by locomotives 41241 and 30072 and ran non stop to Oxenhope. The initial passenger service consisted of seven trains on a Saturday and five on a Sunday.

It had at one time been the declared intention of the society to employ sufficient staff to allow the operation of a Monday to Friday commuter service but after 6½ years without trains no attempt was made to achieve this aim. The overwhelming proportion of the weekend passengers are tourists and, gradually, a summer weekday service has been introduced which is also geared to the tourist market. The railway is scheduled to operate daily for ten weeks during the summer of 1979 and at weekends and bank holidays during the rest of the year. The summer service consists of four trains each way on Mondays to Fridays, seven on Saturdays and thirteen on Sundays. A very restricted service is operated at weekends from November to February with no trains at all on Sundays between Keighley and Haworth. It is estimated that the number of passengers carried has since 1975 exceeded the level of 1961, the last year of B.R. operation, although the nature of the traffic is very different. Damems station was reopened and along with Ingrow is operated as a request stop.

The railway is operated almost exclusively by volunteer members of the preservation society. There is one full time employee and about half a dozen seasonal ones each summer. The continued growth in leisure time has both expanded the tourist potential of the railway and afforded its operating members the free time necessary to work the services.

Under the new management the branch line had to be worked as a self contained unit. Because motive power used to be housed in a small shed alongside the main line at Keighley, it was necessary to develop the former goods yards at Haworth and Oxenhope to accommodate the locomotives and rolling stock respectively. It became apparent by 1971 that the summer Sunday and bank holiday traffic could not be accommodated within the existing line capacity and a passing loop was constructed at what became known as Damems Junction. The site was chosen in preference to Oakworth where there had been a loop in the past because extra land would have been required for a second platform, the old loop having been only for goods traffic. The signal box controlling movements at Damems Junction was formerly at Frizinghall. In 1976 the lease at Keighley station was extended to include platform three.

The motive power and rolling stock is detailed in the 'stock book' published by the preservation society. The size of the locomotive fleet partly reflects the desire of members of the society to preserve as wide a range of locomotives as possible. Since engines can be out of traffic for repairs for considerable lengths of time the available motive power rarely exceeds that required by traffic during the summer. Most of the rolling stock is owned by the railway company or the society but some locomotives and carriages are preserved by private owners. Passenger services are operated by steam trains or, at quiet times, by a diesel railcar.

### A description of the line

Worth Valley trains leave from platform four at Keighley and immediately start to climb at 1 in 58 on a sharp curve. The special opening train in 1867 was the first one to stick at this point but by no means the last, and the line often has to be sanded when the rails are wet. In former times, heavy goods trains were able to set back towards Skipton and take a run at the ascent. The track is now single from Keighley station, the double track like most other remains of the former Great Northern line having been removed. The G.N.R. goods station, which can be seen from the Worth Valley train, has become an Electricity Board depot. Having turned through more than ninety degrees, the train then sets a course towards Ingrow and the gradient becomes easier.

Ingrow station is little used nowadays; the buildings are mostly demolished and it is an unstaffed request stop. The goods shed still stands and is used for locomotive repairs. The tunnel mouth is at the end of the platform; on emerging from the tunnel the train hits the steepest gradient on the line at 1 in 56. To the right is Clough's Mill which was once served by a private siding. The scenery becomes less industrial as the train climbs towards Damems where the short platform now contains only one building, a small signalbox formerly at Earby, between Skipton and Colne. This

One of the two diesel railbuses used by the Keighley & Worth Valley Railway, No. E79962, at Oxenhope in August 1976. (Martin Bairstow).

A Derby-built diesel unit pauses at Haworth in October 1961 during the short period of BR diesel operation of this branch. (M.H. Davison).

Ex-Midland Railway 0-4-4T No. 58066 with the push-pull train at Oxenhope in September 1958. (M.H. Davison).

The tiny station at Damems, closed in 1949 but in use again when this view was taken in June 1973. (Stuart Baker).

Midland 4F No. 3924 arrives at Haworth in July 1975 with a Keighley - Oxenhope train. (D.J. Fowler).

A view probably dating back to Great Northern Railway days, showing Keighley - Halifax and Halifax - Bradford trains connecting at Queensbury. (collection of Roy Brook).

N1 No. 69467 calls at Ingrow with the 6.45 p.m. from Keighley, the last train to Halifax, on May 21st, 1955—the final day of passenger services on the Queensbury lines. (Roy Brook).

The same locomotive at Cullingworth on the same day. (Roy Brook).

N1 No. 69464 on arrival at Keighley with a train from Bradford (Exchange) on a wintry day in February 1955. (John Oxley).

The amply-proportioned Great Northern Railway goods depot at Keighley, February 1955. (John Oxley).

The Queensbury triangle: N1 No. 69467 on a Keighley - Halifax train in May 1955.
(John Oxley).

The St. Dunstans triangle: No. D3547 takes the curve avoiding Bradford with a train
from City Road to Laisterdyke in July 1972. The Lancashire & Yorkshire line is in
the foreground. (Stuart Baker).

On September 7th, 1964, a diesel unit visited Thornton on a railtour. It is seen crossing Thornton viaduct on the return journey. (Stanley King).

Hewenden viaduct stands as a monument to the railway long after its closure. (Stuart Baker).

**A Keighley horse tram about 1898. (collection of Stanley King).**

**The centre of Keighley tramway system—the Mechanics Institute about 1920. (Keighley News).**

controls the signals which protect the level crossing over an unmade road. Beyond the crossing the track doubles for the length of the passing loop and then curves through a cutting until Oakworth comes into view. This station is situated about half a mile from the centre of the village which is reached by a steep hill. There is a level crossing and there used to be a passing loop running through the station. The goods yard is now used for permanent way materials.

On the 1892 alignment beyond Oakworth the width of the embankment and bridges are a reminder that double track was once a possibility. The Vale Mill dam, which the railway originally crossed on a viaduct, is on the left. At this point the railway crosses the river Worth for the last time and for the remainder of the journey follows the valley of the Bridgehouse beck. Haworth station is situated at the foot of the village which is reached by the footbridge outside the station. Immediately beyond this bridge, there was once a level crossing carrying a cobbled road across the line. On the left are the extensive sidings where most of the motive power is now housed. Part of the one time passing loop survives to give access to the yard. Oxenhope appears very much as it did a century ago except that the former goods yard is now given over to carriage sidings and sheds. From Keighley the line has climbed 330 feet at an average gradient of 1 in 76, and unfitted goods trains are warned to stop and pin down their brakes before leaving Oxenhope.

# 4. The Queensbury Lines

## The background

The first railway to serve Halifax was a branch of the Manchester & Leeds opened from Greetland on July 1st, 1844. Proposals to build a line between Halifax and Bradford were mentioned in chapter one because it seemed possible in the mid 1840s that the Manchester company would be connected to the Leeds & Bradford Railway but in 1846 the Manchester & Leeds and the Leeds & Bradford Railways broke off their amalgamation and, literally, went their separate ways. The Manchester & Leeds, which changed its name in 1847 to the Lancashire & Yorkshire Railway, pressed ahead with its West Riding extensions. A rail link between Halifax and Bradford was established on August 7th, 1850. The Bradford terminus was at the Exchange station although that name was not used until 1867.

The distance between Halifax and Bradford by this line is eight miles of which more than 2½ miles are in tunnel. There is a viaduct between Lightcliffe and Wyke whilst the descent from Bowling tunnel to the terminus is at 1 in 50. When considering the engineering features of the later route via Queensbury it is worth remembering that this earlier line is far from devoid of earthworks and gradients. The line had proved expensive and the Lancashire & Yorkshire Railway was unable to carry its West Riding lines any further. Parliamentary approval existed for a line to Leeds which would have given the company its desired independent route to that city as well as providing the 'short line' between Leeds and Bradford. On the day that the Lancashire & Yorkshire obtained an Act to abandon its Leeds to Bradford powers a new company was incorporated under the title of the Leeds, Bradford & Halifax Junction Railway to build the same line. On August 1st, 1854, this railway was opened from Leeds Central to Bradford Adolphus Street and to Bowling Junction where it joined the Bradford - Halifax line. It was worked and later taken over by the Great Northern Railway which was granted running powers from Bowling Junction to Halifax in return for Lancashire & Yorkshire trains running from Bowling Junction to Leeds Central. On January 7th, 1867, the Great Northern Railway began to share Bradford

Exchange station having opened the connecting line between Hammerton Street Junction and Mill Lane Junction.

To the west of the Bradford - Halifax line the lie of the land becomes much more difficult, the plateau at over 1,000 feet being broken by steep sided valleys. The town of Queensbury stands at 1,150 feet. Assisted by supplies of local coal the weaving industry flourished here, the best known firm being John Foster & Sons at Black Dyke Mills. Another high lying woollen township is Denholme at almost 1,000 feet. These towns together with Clayton and Thornton lay on the frontier of the sphere of influence of the Lancashire & Yorkshire, Great Northern and Midland Railways.

## The Halifax & Ovenden Junction Railway

The station at Halifax lies at the bottom of the town. A temporary structure on the present site was opened on the day the Bradford line opened in 1850. Previously the terminus of the branch from Greetland had been at Shaw Syke, half a mile to the south. Both the Lancashire & Yorkshire and the Great Northern companies were concerned about the difficulty of transporting goods from the higher parts of the town and about the congestion at Halifax station. They may have seen a line up the Ovenden Valley as a possible springboard for future expansion but were quite prepared to support it as an end in itself in order to establish goods facilities at North Bridge and Holmfield from where a good deal of traffic was being carted by road to Halifax station.

The Halifax & Ovenden Junction Railway was incorporated on June 30th, 1864. It was authorised to commence at a triangular junction with the Lancashire & Yorkshire Railway between Halifax station and Beacon Hill tunnel, and to run for 2¾ miles to Holmfield. The authorised capital was £90,000 of which the Lancashire & Yorkshire and Great Northern companies had each agreed to subscribe £30,000. Five years were allowed for completion and it was agreed that the two main line companies would operate the line jointly.

Extensions of time were granted by Parliament in 1867, 1870 and 1873. The 1867 Act doubled the authorised capital whilst that of 1870 vested the line jointly in the two companies who were empowered to purchase the minority shareholdings. Preliminary work involved demolishing property to make way for the viaduct between Halifax and North Bridge and the construction of a new bridge at the latter point with adequate clearance for the new railway. Opening to goods traffic was finally achieved on August 17th, 1874, as far as North Bridge and to Holmfield two weeks later on Tuesday, September 1st.

## The Bradford and Thornton Railway

Separate proposals for a branch line to Thornton were advanced in 1865 by the Lancashire & Yorkshire and the Great Northern Railways. The two railways agreed to amalgamate their plans and to build the line at a cost of £40,000 to each company. No Act was obtained and the proposal failed. Business interests in the locality were frustrated at the failure of the main line companies to serve their area. In 1870 they promoted the Bradford & Thornton Railway to build a line which, because of the involvement of Queensbury firms, was to pass as near as possible to that town. John Foster & Sons, in evidence to Parliament, expressed the fear that local supplies of coal would run out and pointed to the difficulties of getting supplies from elsewhere by road.

The Bradford & Thornton scheme was supported by the Great Northern Railway who agreed to subscribe half the cost. With the aid of the Great Northern and despite opposition from the Lancashire & Yorkshire Railway, the line was authorised by Act of Parliament on July 24th, 1871. The new railway was to commence at a triangular junction with the recently opened Hammerton Street Junction to Mill Lane Junction line and was to run for 5½ miles to Thornton. A branch, 1¼ miles in length, was to be built to provide goods facilities to the area around City Road. An Act of July 18th, 1872, amalgamated the Bradford & Thornton Railway with the Great Northern.

The earthworks on the Thornton line were heavy and construction took six years. The first opening, on December 4th, 1876, was to goods traffic only and involved the sections to Great Horton and to City Road. Extension to Clayton followed in July 1877 and to Thornton, after completion of Clayton tunnel and Thornton viaduct, on May 1st 1878. It was predicted in the 'Halifax Courier' that the price of coal in Thornton would fall by 2s. 6d or 3s. per ton. The line opened to passengers on October 14th, 1878 and the initial timetable provided five trains on weekdays from Bradford Exchange and two from Laisterdyke to Thornton. These served stations at Manchester Road, Great Horton and Clayton. The frequency from Bradford was soon increased but the through Laisterdyke to Thornton passenger workings were shortlived. Convenient connections between the Leeds and Thornton lines became available on the opening of St. Dunstans station which first appeared in 'Bradshaw', for Thornton trains only, in January 1879 and for the Leeds line in the following May edition.

### The Halifax, Thornton & Keighley Railway

In 1864 an unsuccessful bid was made to promote the Halifax, Huddersfield & Keighley Railway. Amongst the promoters were influential local businessmen including Isaac Holden, the chairman of the Keighley & Worth Valley Railway. The objects of this scheme included shortening the route between Huddersfield and

Halifax, providing a more convenient station in Halifax and establishing a link with the Midland Railway at Keighley. The continuing failure to provide a rail link across Bradford made a direct line to Keighley of particular interest to Halifax.

Undeterred by their initial failure the supporters of this line tried again in 1867 and this time gained the support of the Midland Railway when their Bill came before the House of Commons, only to see the Midland withdraw support in the House of Lords due to other capital commitments. In 1872 the Midland Railway was again approached but declined support advising the promoters to press ahead on their own. They tried the Great Northern Railway which expressed no interest in Huddersfield but said it would join in a Halifax to Keighley project if half the cost was subscribed locally. The line was to commence at Holmfield as a continuation of the Halifax & Ovenden Junction Railway and join the Bradford & Thornton by a triangular junction at Queensbury. Continuing from Thornton the Great Northern proposed an independent terminus in Keighley. The promoters included the Foster family of Queensbury and John Fraser who was the engineer to the Bradford & Thornton Railway.

The Bill was opposed by the Lancashire & Yorkshire, Midland and Keighley & Worth Valley Railways. The Midland won over some of the supporters of the Bill by promising, in the event of its defeat, to revive the Huddersfield, Halifax and Keighley line which many Halifax people favoured. The royal assent was nevertheless granted on August 5th, 1873. The Midland Railway, which had hitherto shown no more interest in the Queensbury area than any other main line company, now appeared to resent the Great Northern gaining control of the territory. In November 1873, it deposited a Bill for a line from Huddersfield through a high level station in Halifax and then passing to the west of Holmfield and Queensbury and joining the existing Midland line with a triangular junction between Manningham and Bradford. There was little support for this proposal because it did not meet Bradford's demands for a through railway and it would have been even less convenient for Queensbury than the newly authorised Great Northern line which it would have crossed between Queensbury and Thornton.

Another hopeless proposal, advanced in 1876, was the work of John Fraser. The West Riding & Lancashire Railway was to leave the Midland by a triangular junction between Manningham and Bradford whence it was to climb at 1 in 56 to join the Great Northern at City Road. With the help of an additional curve to give direct running towards Queensbury the West Riding & Lancashire would stick with the Great Northern to Holmfield and then, after serving a high level Halifax station, would proceed in two branches to Huddersfield and Manchester. The Midland

Railway was not interested in this scheme which never got off the ground.

Opening of the line between Queensbury and Holmfield depended on progress in constructing Queensbury tunnel and Strines cutting which together occupied most of the 2¼ miles. Difficulties arose with water bearing strata but these were overcome in time for the line to be opened to goods traffic on October 14th, 1878, the same day that the Thornton line opened for passengers. A station, built to serve Queensbury at the Bradford side of the triangular junction, was opened on Easter Saturday 1879. Passenger services to Halifax commenced on December 1st, 1879. Initially trains ran non-stop from Queensbury but a temporary station was provided at Holmfield within a fortnight. By providing passenger facilities at North Bridge it was intended to serve parts of the town for which Halifax station was inconvenient. Although incomplete, North Bridge station opened on March 25th, 1880, whilst agitation for a station to serve Ovenden met with success in June 1881. The Great Northern Railway provided the only passenger service over the joint line from Halifax to Holmfield but the Lancashire & Yorkshire operated its share of the goods trains from the opening in 1874.

**Progress to Keighley**

A feature of the nineteenth century was the trade cycle by which periods of rapid growth, full employment, trade surpluses and inflation alternated with periods of stagnation, unemployment, and falling prices. The process was largely self regulating because there was no Government management of the ecomony in those days. The effect on railway construction was that projects commenced in boom times sometimes took a long time to complete in changed economic circumstances. The line from Thornton to Keighley was a very expensive project because of the earthworks required. The Great Northern Railway carried out the work slowly and it was not until September 1st, 1882, that a single line was available for goods traffic as far as Denholme.

In the interests of economy the proposal for an independent passenger terminus at Keighley was dropped. This move met with the approval of the local authorities who had urged the Great Northern and Midland companies to come to some arrangement for a joint station. By an agreement of June 1st, 1881, the Midland Railway undertook to double the track of the Worth Valley branch as far as a junction with the proposed Great Northern line so that passenger trains from Bradford Exchange and Halifax would be able to use a new station which was to be built jointly. This arrangement fitted in with the existing need for the Midland Railway to improve its passenger facilities at Keighley. The new station was opened on Sunday May 6th, 1883, the first train to use it being the 12.30 p.m. from Oxenhope. The junction between the main line and the Worth Valley branch was realigned so as to allow separate platforms to be provided for the branch line which would later be used by the Great Northern Railway also. The new station is situated on the south side of Bradford Road which, since 1879, has been carried over the railway by a bridge. The previous level crossing had been the subject of complaint by the Keighley Local Board for some years. The old station, to the north of Bradford Road, was quickly demolished.

By 1884 work was sufficiently advanced for services to be extended. On January 1st, 1884, the 6.10 a.m. from Bradford Exchange was the first passenger train to run beyond Thornton, thus opening the service to Denholme. Traffic began running through to Keighley goods depot on April 1st, but it was not yet possible to run onto the Midland Railway to gain access to the passenger station. As an interim measure, eight passenger trains per day began running to Ingrow from Monday, April 7th. No attempt was made to time these trains to connect with the Worth Valley service during this period and so passengers would have to make their own way into Keighley until the trains were finally extended there on November 1st, 1884. The initial service from Keighley consisted of 18 departures on weekdays and four on Sundays. Evidence that the town was now served by the Great Northern Railway came with the introduction of cheap excursions to Lincoln, Boston and Skegness.

The railway passed through the centre of Cullingworth and a station was provided here at the opening. The line passed no nearer than within two miles of Wilsden but, after providing road access from the relatively nearby village of Harecroft, the Great Northern opened a station called Wilsden on July 1st, 1886. The question of a station at Cross Roads seems to have been discussed. The village lies above Lees Moor tunnel and a station would have had to be sited at the Ingrow end overlooking the Worth Valley. Even though the Great Northern thought it might pick up some of the traffic then going to Haworth, by the Midland Railway, the Cross Roads proposal was not taken up.

**Queensbury Station**

Situated at the focal point of the Great Northern lines between Bradford, Halifax and Keighley, this station was renowned not only for its unusual construction but for its remoteness. The town of Queensbury could claim to be the most important along the route. Its principal industrialists had supported the construction of the railway and had influenced the route from Bradford to Thornton so as to pass as close as practical to Queensbury. The distance from the town to the station was one mile and the difference in altitude about 400 feet. Prior to the advent of motor

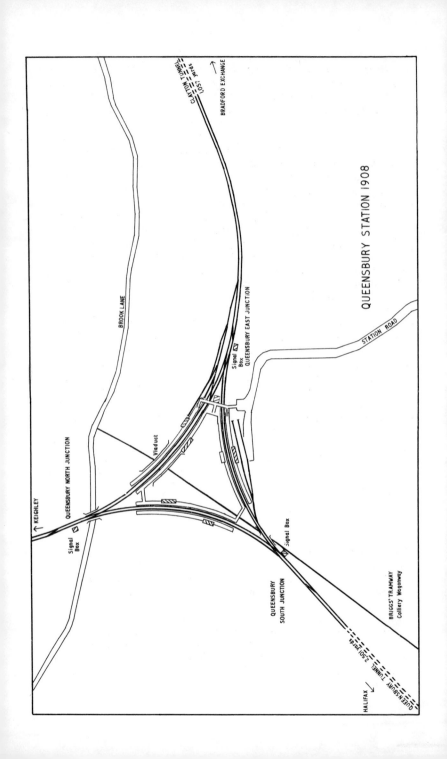

QUEENSBURY STATION 1908

transport this would have been insufficient an obstacle to have prevented rail traffic developing. The complaints against the Great Northern Railway by the inhabitants of Queensbury did not arise from the location of the station because they probably accepted that it had to be on the railway line. When the line opened in 1878 there was no station at Queensbury until a temporary structure was thrown together for Easter 1879. This had no goods facilities, no access for vehicles and the only footpath was unmade and unlit.

On January 3rd, 1882, the Queensbury Local Board asked the Great Northern Railway what it proposed to do on the question of road access to the station. The company replied that alterations to the station might be required when the line to Keighley opened and proposed that action be deferred. The Local Board asked that, as an interim measure, the footpath should be provided with gas lamps. The railway replied in April that there was no urgency for this now that it was summer. On September 5th the Local Board pointed out that it would soon be winter again. A year later some lights had been provided but local opinion doubted whether they were enough. In February 1884 the Great Northern Railway proposed a road from the town to the station and subsequently asked the Local Board to contribute to the cost. The Queensbury Local Board replied that they would not spend ratepayers' money on a road which only led to a railway station and which for the greater part of its length lay outside the Queensbury district boundary. They informed the railway 'That the inhabitants of this locality are very indignant at the treatment they have hitherto received from the Great Northern Company for, while other villages on the route are provided with good roads to the station, Queensbury is entirely neglected although it should be the most important'.

This dialogue continued for several more years but the Great Northern Railway was not entirely inactive. In 1885 an engineers' report showed that it would be possible to construct a new station with platforms on all three sides of the triangular junction. As for communication with the town two alternative forms of rail link were discussed. The cheapest alternative at £17,500 was for a rope-worked incline at a gradient of 1 in 6. A more satisfactory alternative but at double the cost was a circuitous route, two miles in length with a maximum gradient of 1 in 30. In 1888 the Great Northern Board resolved to press ahead with the latter idea if half the cost could be raised locally. John Foster & Sons, who favoured the circuitous locomotive worked line, advised that trade was bad and went on to blame the lack of railway facilities for this fact.

Work commenced on the new station in 1889 and a road to the town was included in the plans. The station opened on January 1st, 1890, and the road came into use soon afterwards. No action was taken on the question of a branch line but sidings were provided. In 1895 consideration was given to the suitability of Briggs' tramway for connection to and use by the railway. This was a track used for rope-hauling coal from the mine near Queensbury station to the town. No action was taken. On February 17th, 1896, the Great Northern directors visited Queensbury and soon afterwards a few more lights were provided on Station Road and poster boards erected at the top of the road together with a signpost in the form of a hand pointing to the station. These appear to have represented the ultimate in Queensbury's railway facilities! In 1901 electric tramways were opened to the centre of the town from both Bradford and Halifax and soon began to make inroads into Great Northern passenger traffic.

## Train services

Until the British Railways period it was often difficult to differentiate between through trains and connections in the public timetable. This means that it is practically impossible to tell whether a train from Bradford Exchange ran through to Halifax with a connection for Keighley or whether the train ran to Keighley with a connection for Halifax. The author's grandparents, occasional passengers between Horton Park and Halifax, used to see which way the train turned at Queensbury and act accordingly. At certain times of the day trains stood on all three sides of the triangle allowing connections to be made in all directions. For example, the 1910 timetable shows arrivals at 10.26, 10.30 and 10.31 a.m. from Bradford Exchange, Halifax and Keighley followed by departures at 10.33 to Keighley, 10.35 to Bradford Exchange and 10.36 to Halifax.

At that time there were 22 weekday departures from Bradford Exchange to Halifax or Keighley. In most cases the other of these places could be reached by changing at Queensbury. There were 21 trains from Halifax for the Queensbury line and 16 starting from Keighley. On Sundays nine trains left Bradford Exchange for Halifax or Keighley. The journey from Bradford to Halifax by this route took between 35 and 40 minutes depending on the number of stops and the duration of the wait at Queensbury. This was slower than by the alternative Lancashire & Yorkshire service which was more frequent. A Great Northern train from Bradford to Keighley took 45 minutes, twice as long as the faster trains by the Midland Railway from Forster Square.

Whilst the railways held a monopoly over the available traffic the Queensbury lines prospered, despite their disadvantages against the older railways and the inconvenient location of some of the stations. Some traffic was lost to the electric tramways after the turn of the century. The Bradford trams began to eat into the traffic at stations as far as Thornton, whilst Ovenden, Holmfield and Queensbury became prey to the Halifax tramways. As we shall

66

see in the next chapter, Ingrow gained a tram service to Keighley which not only made the combined frequency of the Midland and Great Northern trains look appalling but ran direct to Keighley town centre. Due to the way the tramways were planned the erosion of railway traffic was limited to local passengers. They carried no freight whilst the break of gauge between the Bradford and Halifax systems kept them from seriously entering the market for longer distance traffic. The two systems met at Queensbury, Shelf and Bailiff Bridge but the Halifax gauge was 3 ft. 6 in and that of Bradford 4 ft. Two further different gauges were used in Leeds and Huddersfield. The tramways could not kill the Queensbury lines and, indeed, they succumbed to the advance of motor transport long before the railway.

## Decline and closure

The Queensbury lines were particularly badly placed to face the threat of motor transport. The inconvenience of Queensbury and Wilsden stations was legendary whilst other railway lines had always catered for the greater share of traffic from Bradford to Halifax and Keighley. Only for Halifax to Keighley traffic was the Great Northern line the sole rail link because of the failure of all schemes to connect the two terminal stations in Bradford. In retrospect it does not seem too surprising that the Queensbury lines were caught relatively early in the onslaught of closures after nationalisation of British Railways.

In contrast to the depleted services which were operated on the former Midland lines in West Yorkshire in the post war years, the Queensbury lines appeared practically immune from cuts. There had been no Sunday service since 1938 but the weekday frequency remained at pre-war levels. In 1950 the number of peak hour departures from Bradford was increased but some off peak and evening trains were withdrawn and the number of through trains from Keighley to Halifax was reduced. A number of station stops were eliminated, particularly at Queensbury which lost much of its importance as an interchange station because none of the remaining Keighley to Halifax trains were booked to stop.

The first post-war closures affected the two stations nearest to Bradford. St. Dunstans was used as an interchange station and its closure in 1952 meant that passengers would henceforth have to change at Bradford Exchange. Traffic originating at St. Dunstans in its own right was light. Closed at the same time was Horton Park, 1½ miles by rail from Bradford but well within walking distance by road and served by frequent buses. The adjacent cricket and football ground provided this station with much of its passenger traffic and it was occasionally used for this purpose after the regular trains ceased to stop.

In 1954 B.R. announced that it would save £48,000 per annum if

L.N.E.R.

## WEEKDAYS

| | | A a.m | B a.m | A a.m | A a.m | B a.m | A a.m | B a.m | A a.m | B 12.10 | A 12.50 | B 1.30 | B 3.30 | B 4 | B 5 | B 5.45 | A 6.00 | A 6.46 | pm | A 9.15 | B 10.27 | pm 11.20 |
|---|---|---|---|---|---|---|---|---|---|---|---|---|---|---|---|---|---|---|---|---|---|---|
| BRADFORD EXCHANGE | dep | 5 45 | 5 55 | 6 30 | 7 15 | 7 54 | 9 03 | 10 08 | 12 10 | 12 50 | 1 30 | 3 30 | 4 38 | 5 15 | 5 45 | 6 00 | 6 46 | | 9 15 | 10 27 | 11 20 |
| ST DUNSTANS | | 5 49 | 5 58 | 6 35 | 7 20 | 7 58 | 9 06 | 10 11 | 12 13 | 12 53 | 1 36 | 3 34 | 4 41 | 5 18 | 5 48 | — | 6 49 | | 9 19 | 10 31 | — |
| HORTON PARK | | 5 53 | 6 03 | 6 39 | 7 24 | 8 02 | 9 09 | 10 15 | 12 16 | 12 57 | 1 40 | 3 38 | 4 45 | 5 22 | 5 52 | 6 06 | 6 53 | | | | — |
| GREAT HORTON | | 5 56 | 6 07 | 6 42 | 7 27 | 8 05 | 9 13 | 10 18 | 12 20 | 1 00 | 1 43 | 3 45 | 4 52 | 5 25 | 5 55 | 6 09 | 6 56 | | 9 25 | 10 34 | — |
| CLAYTON | | 6 00 | 6 12 | 6 46 | 7 31 | 8 09 | 9 17 | 10 22 | 12 24 | 1 04 | 1 47 | 3 49 | 4 56 | 5 29 | 5 59 | 6 13 | 7 00 | | 9 29 | 10 38 | — |
| QUEENSBURY | arr | 6 04 | 6 17 | 6 50 | 7 35 | 8 13 | 9 21 | 10 26 | 12 28 | 1 08 | 1 51 | 3 49 | 4 56 | 5 33 | 6 03 | 6 17 | 7 04 | | 9 30 | 10 42 | — |
| QUEENSBURY | dep | | 6 18 | 6N55 | | 8N18 | 9 25 | 10N35 | 12 29 | | 1 52 | 3N54 | 5N00 | 5 37 | | 6 07 | | 8N08 | | 10 49 | — |
| THORNTON | | | 6 22 | 6 59 | | 8 22 | 9 29 | 10 39 | 12 33 | | 1 56 | 3 58 | 5 04 | 5 41 | | 6 11 | | 8 12 | | 10 53 | — |
| DENHOLME | | | 6 25 | 7 02 | | 8 25 | 9 32 | 10 42 | 12 36 | | 1 59 | 4 01 | 5 07 | 5 44 | | 6 14 | | 8 16 | | 10 56 | — |
| WILSDEN | | | 6 29 | 7 05 | | 8 28 | 9 35 | 10 45 | 12 39 | | 2 02 | 4 04 | 5 10 | 5 47 | | 6 17 | | 8 18 | | 10 59 | — |
| CULLINGWORTH | | | 6 32 | 7 09 | | 8 31 | 9 38 | 10 48 | 12 42 | | 2 05 | 4 07 | 5 13 | 5 50 | | 6 20 | | 8 18 | | 11 02 | — |
| INGROW | | | 6 39 | 7 16 | | 8 38 | 9 45 | 10 55 | 12 49 | | 2 14 | 4 14 | 5 20 | 5 57 | | 6 27 | | 8 20 | | 11 09 | — |
| KEIGHLEY | arr | | 6 42 | 7 19 | | 8 41 | 9 48 | 10 58 | 12 52 | | 2 15 | 4 17 | 5 23 | 6 00 | | 6 30 | | 8 20 | | 11 12 | — |
| QUEENSBURY | dep | 6 07 | | 6 57 | 7 38 | 8 15 | 9N26 | 10 34 | 12N32 | 1 15 | | 3 52 | 5 04 | 5N37 | | | 6 18 | 7 08 | 9 37 | 10N51 | — |
| HOLMFIELD | | 6 11 | | 7 02 | 7 42 | 8 19 | 9 30 | 10 39 | 12 36 | 1 19 | | 3 56 | 5 08 | 5 41 | | | 6 21 | 7 12 | 9 41 | 10 55 | — |
| OVENDEN | | 6 13 | | 7 04 | 7 44 | 8 21 | 9 32 | 10 40 | 12 38 | 1 21 | | 3 58 | 5 11 | 5 43 | | | 6 24 | 7 16 | 9 43 | 10 57 | — |
| NORTH BRIDGE | | 6 17 | | 7 08 | 7 48 | 8 25 | 9 36 | 10 44 | 12 42 | 1 25 | | 4 02 | 5 16 | 5 47 | | | 6 28 | 7 18 | 9 47 | 11 01 | — |
| HALIFAX | arr | 6 19 | | 7 10 | 7 50 | 8 27 | 9 38 | 10 46 | 12 44 | 1 27 | | 4 05 | 5 18 | 5 49 | | | 6 30 | 7 20 | 9 49 | 11 03 | 11 43 |

## WEEKDAYS

| | | B a.m 6N35 | B a.m | A a.m 8 20 | B a.m 7N50 | A a.m 9 05 | a.m 10N12 | pm 12 03 | B pm | A pm 1 17 | B pm | B pm 3N35 | B pm | A pm 5 43 | A pm 5 10 | A pm 6 00 | B pm | B pm | A pm 7 50 | A pm 10 25 |
|---|---|---|---|---|---|---|---|---|---|---|---|---|---|---|---|---|---|---|---|---|---|
| HALIFAX | dep | 6 38 | — | 8 20 | 7N50 | 9 05 | 10N12 | 12 03 | | 1 17 | | 3N35 | 4N41 | 5 43 | 5 10 | 6 00 | | | 7 50 | 10 25 |
| NORTH BRIDGE | | 6 42 | — | 8 23 | 7 53 | 9 08 | 10 15 | 12 06 | | 1 20 | | 3 38 | 4 44 | 5 46 | 5 13 | 6 03 | | | 7 53 | 10 28 |
| OVENDEN | | 6 45 | — | 8 27 | 7 57 | 9 12 | 10 19 | 12 10 | | 1 24 | | 3 42 | 4 48 | 5 50 | 5 16 | 6 06 | | | 7 57 | 10 32 |
| HOLMFIELD | | 6 48 | — | 8 30 | 8 00 | 9 15 | 10 22 | 12 13 | | 1 27 | | 3 45 | 4 51 | 5 53 | 5 20 | 6 09 | | | 8 00 | 10 35 |
| QUEENSBURY | arr | 6 51 | — | 8 36 | 8 08 | 9 21 | 10 28 | 12 19 | | 1 33 | | 3 51 | 4 57 | 5 59 | 5 26 | 6 12 | | | 8 06 | 10 41 |
| KEIGHLEY | dep | 6 25 | 7 05 | 8 37 | 7 37 | 8N52 | 10 01 | 11N50 | 12 42 | | | 4N28 | 4N55 | | 4N41 | | 5 46 | | 7N27 | 10N15 |
| INGROW | | 6 29 | 7 11 | 8 43 | 7 43 | 8 58 | 10 06 | 11 56 | 12 48 | | | 4 34 | 5 01 | | | | 5 52 | 6 31 | 7 33 | 10 21 |
| CULLINGWORTH | | 6 39 | 7 19 | 8 51 | 7 51 | 9 06 | 10 13 | 12 04 | 12 56 | | | 4 42 | 5 09 | | | | 6 05 | 6 45 | 7 41 | 10 29 |
| WILSDEN | | 6 43 | 7 23 | 8 55 | 7 55 | 9 10 | 10 19 | 12 08 | | | | 4 46 | 5 13 | | | | 6 08 | 6 49 | 7 45 | 10 34 |
| DENHOLME | | 6 46 | 7 26 | 8 58 | 7 58 | 9 13 | 10 22 | 12 11 | 1 03 | | | 4 49 | 5 17 | | | | 6 11 | 6 52 | 7 48 | 10 37 |
| THORNTON | | 6 50 | 7 30 | 9 02 | 8 02 | 9 17 | 10 26 | 12 15 | 1 07 | | | 4 53 | 5 20 | | | | 6 16 | 6 56 | 7 52 | 10 41 |
| QUEENSBURY | arr | 6 53 | 7 33 | 9 05 | 8 05 | 9 20 | 10 29 | 12 18 | | | | 4 56 | 5 23 | | | | 6 17 | 6 59 | 7 55 | 10 44 |
| QUEENSBURY | dep | 6 57 | 7 34 | 8 37 | 8N52 | 9 25 | 10 32 | 12 21 | 1 16 | 1 35 | | 3 56 | 5 27 | 5 03 | 6 00 | 6 17 | 6 17 | 7 07 | 8 09 | 10 50 |
| CLAYTON | | 7 02 | 7 37 | 8 40 | 8 18 | 9 28 | 10 35 | 12 25 | 1 19 | 1 38 | | 3 59 | 5 30 | 5 06 | 6 03 | 6 20 | 6 20 | 7 10 | 8 12 | 10 53 |
| GREAT HORTON | | 7 05 | 7 40 | 8 43 | 8 21 | — | 10 38 | 12 28 | 1 22 | 1 41 | | 4 02 | 5 33 | 5 09 | 6 06 | 6 23 | 6 23 | 7 13 | 8 15 | 10 56 |
| HORTON PARK | | 7 07 | 7 42 | 8 45 | 8 23 | — | 10 40 | 12 31 | 1 24 | 1 43 | | 4 05 | 5 35 | 5 12 | 6 09 | 6 25 | 6 25 | 7 15 | 8 17 | — |
| ST DUNSTANS | | 7 11 | 7 46 | 8 49 | 8 26 | 10 37 | 10 44 | 12 34 | 1 28 | 1 47 | | 4 09 | 5 39 | 5 16 | 6 12 | 6 30 | 6 30 | 7 19 | 8 21 | — |
| BRADFORD EXCHANGE | arr | 7 14 | 7 49 | 8 52 | 8 29 | 8 37 | 10 47 | 12 37 | 1 31 | 1 50 | | 4 12 | 5 42 | 5 19 | 6 15 | 6 35 | 6 35 | 7 28 | 8 24 | 11 04 |

NO SUNDAY SERVICE

A – Through train between BRADFORD EXCHANGE and HALIFAX
B – Through train between BRADFORD EXCHANGE and KEIGHLEY
N – Through train between KEIGHLEY and HALIFAX

JULY 1947

the Transport Users Consultative Committee accepted its proposal to withdraw all passenger services between Bradford Exchange, Halifax and Keighley via Queensbury. The T.U.C.C. accepted the B.R. case after the usual public hearing into objections and the last day of service was fixed for Saturday, May 21st, 1955. The residents of Harecroft continued their protest for, although Wilsden station was a good walk from the village along a purpose built road like that at Queensbury, it provided their only public transport. The new Prime Minister, Sir Anthony Eden, called a general election for Thursday, May 26th. Suddenly the plight of this handful of travellers at Harecroft found a voice in the candidates of both persuasions in the constituencies of Shipley, Bradford South, Halifax and Keighley. These last two seats are particularly marginal. Supporters of the railway apparently couldn't lose because both parties were pledged to do all they could to save the line if elected. None of this interfered with the planned closure date.

On December 16th, 1955, the Member for Shipley introduced a debate in the House of Commons. He was supported by members for the neighbouring constituencies and asked for reinstatement of the passenger service. He called for a service of diesel multiple units which had, the previous year, been introduced between Bradford Exchange and Leeds Central upon which service they had proved successful in attracting traffic. In reply the Minister offered no hope of a revived passenger service and indicated that B.R. foresaw further cash savings in closing parts of the line to goods traffic also. It could be argued that the Queensbury lines were hardly a priority for the new trains, so desperately required to improve local services elsewhere, but B.R. failed to strengthen their case by putting forward the feeble argument that diesel multiple units would be unable to work the gradients which were no worse than on some other West Yorkshire lines.

In May 1955 B.R. stated that all stations on the Queensbury lines would remain open to freight traffic, except Ovenden which had no goods facilities, and that passenger excursions would continue. During the 1955 season a number of such trains ran and served intermediate stations, specially reopened and staffed for the purpose. These ventures were not repeated and, as foreshadowed in the Minister's statement to the House in December, Lees Moor and Queensbury tunnels were closed in May 1956. The route was thus divided into three branch lines: Keighley to Ingrow, Bradford to Cullingworth and Halifax to Holmfield.

Goods trains continued to travel over these sections but, with no effort being made to stem the decline in traffic, the progressive closure of the system took place over the next 18 years. In 1960 B.R. announced that it was no longer viable to convey goods from Halifax via Holmfield to the Halifax High Level line so the route

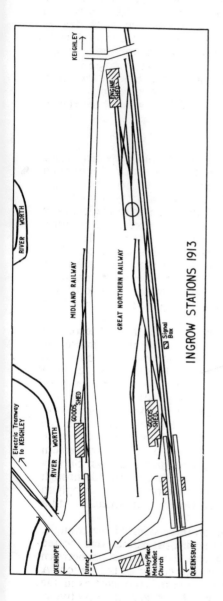

INGROW STATIONS 1913

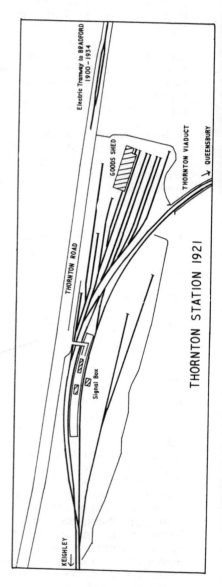

THORNTON STATION 1921

beyond North Bridge was closed. Cullingworth closed in 1963 leaving Thornton as the terminus for two years until the coal trains were withdrawn from there and the line cut back to Horton Park. The coal yard at Ingrow was closed the same day as Thornton but, ironically, this closure facilitated the reopening of the Keighley & Worth Valley Railway. Trains still ran to City Road goods depot and even carried occasional through wagons from Spain until August 1972 when the coal yard at Horton Park also closed. The last section of the Queensbury lines to see traffic was a single track the length of the viaduct at Halifax which carried coal trains to North Bridge until 1974.

## A description of the route

From the Great Northern goods station at Keighley, which closed on July 15th, 1961, the line crossed under the Worth Valley line and into a short tunnel from which it emerged to run parallel with the Midland Railway. At Keighley G.N. Junction a connecting line, which was originally double track but later reduced to single, linked the two systems. Passenger trains, having departed from platform three at Keighley, used this connection to reach the tracks of the Great Northern Railway. Ingrow station stood adjacent to but at a higher level than the Worth Valley station; the engine shed was situated between G.N. Junction and Ingrow. The route continued to climb on the opposite side of the valley to the Oxenhope line, the average gradient from Keighley to Denholme being 1 in 50 but stretches were at 1 in 45.

Lees Moor tunnel turned through more than ninety degrees in its 1,533 yards and had no ventilation. Cullingworth was entered by a 150 yard long viaduct and was conveniently served by a two platform station. The railway crossed the Hewenden Valley on a seventeen arch viaduct, 376 yards long, with a maximum height of 123 feet. Owing to the proximity of Manywells Reservoir it was necessary to sink the stone piers to a depth of 65 feet. The viaduct brought the line into Wilsden station, situated two miles from the place it purported to serve and approached by a road from the village of Harecroft. Denholme station was on the lower, eastern edge of the woollen town overlooking Doe Park Reservoir. Shortly after emerging from Well Head tunnel, the line passed through Thornton station with its island platform before turning sharply to the right to cross Thornton viaduct, a twenty arch structure with a maximum height of 104 feet.

At Queensbury, platforms lined all three sides of the triangle. There were buildings on each but the principal offices were located by the footbridge at the Bradford end. Communication between platforms was by different means at each corner of the station. A footbridge, a narrow subway and a sleeper crossing linked the platforms at the Bradford, Halifax and Keighley ends respectively.

At one time there were signal boxes at all three junctions but, later, the East Junction box was adapted to control the whole area. Beyond the site of the original, much criticised station, the line to Bradford entered Clayton tunnel from which it emerged to run parallel to Pasture Lane and into the island platform station at Clayton. The railway reached Great Horton through a deep cutting and then turned almost through a right angle to run alongside Horton Park Avenue. Horton Park station was situated opposite the cricket and football ground and near to St. Luke's Hospital. Just beyond the station was the junction with the double track branch from City Road goods depot which never carried a passenger service but enabled the railway to serve the many mills in this part of Bradford. Descending at gradients of between 1 in 45 and 1 in 60 the line passed under Manchester Road where the station, closed in 1915, was an island platform structure. After passing through a short tunnel the line then ran under the Lancashire & Yorkshire Bradford to Halifax line to join the G.N.R. Bradford to Leeds line by a triangular junction. St. Dunstans station was built on this junction with platforms on the two sides leading to Bradford. A few yards beyond St. Dunstans the line curves in to join the L. & Y. at Mill Lane Junction. The present Bradford Exchange station was opened in 1973 and is the third structure on the site. For most of their period of operation, the Queensbury trains used the ten platform terminus which was opened in 1887.

Returning to Queensbury, the Halifax line almost immediately entered the 1 mile 741 yard Queensbury tunnel, the second longest on the Great Northern Railway. Strines cutting was 1,033 yards long, 59 feet deep and hewn out of sandstone rock. When the railway was under construction, the Strines beck had to be diverted across the cutting by an aqueduct and this, subsequently, left the line open to the risk of flooding on occasions. On a falling gradient of 1 in 80 the railway entered Holmfield station, the junction for the Halifax High Level branch to St. Pauls opened in 1890 to provide railway facilities to the upper part of the town. The G.N.R. had a shed at Holmfield where there were two platforms plus a bay for the St. Pauls trains. Ovenden station had no facilities for goods and was made of timber. As the line drops in to Halifax it is in a shallow valley which is spanned by North Bridge where the last station, an island platform, was located. From here Halifax is reached by a viaduct of 40 arches, each of 36 foot span. Halifax station had three island platforms and the Great Northern trains used the one nearest the town. The principal buildings were situated on the centre island which was the entrance to the station before it was reconstructed and enlarged in 1886. Since withdrawal of the Queensbury trains, Halifax has seen the progressive reduction of its railway facilities so that only the former Lancashire & Yorkshire service from Leeds and Bradford to Manchester via the Calder Valley remains. Platforms 1 and 2, the island furthest away from the town, serve these whilst the others remain without tracks. The goods yard lies on the town side of the station and is crossed on a bridge by the station approach road.

After closure the track was lifted and the route of the railway began to return to nature. Some sites have been redeveloped, including that of Thornton station which is now a primary school. Queensbury station was sold to become, literally, a rubbish dump. Station Road is still in the news. As recently as January 15th, 1979, the 'Telegraph & Argus' carried a complaint that the new owner doesn't maintain it as well as the railway used to. The tunnels are sealed but Strines cutting remains and the viaducts at Halifax, Thornton, Hewenden and Cullingworth stand as a reminder of what was a magnificent, but expensive, railway.

# 5. The Keighley Corporation Tramways

FOR a period of 35 years, local passenger transport in Keighley was provided by a small street tramway system. The history of this undertaking and of its associated trolley and motor bus services is told by Stanley King in his comprehensive work 'Keighley Corporation Transport'. A brief account of the tramway services is given in this chapter.

Under the Tramways Act, 1870, a company required the support of the local authority before applying for an order authorising the construction of a line. The option of compulsory purchase after 21 years' operation was available to the council, and tramway development was closely influenced by local government boundaries. Prior to 1895, the Borough of Keighley covered an area of about one mile radius. The failure of the tramway system ever to extend beyond this boundary was a severe factor limiting its development. The failure to connect with the Bradford system must have been a principal reason for the early demise of the Keighley tramways.

## The horse trams

Many municipal tramways were laid to the standard railway gauge of 4 ft. 8½ in. and railway wagons were able to be hauled through the streets of some towns. The Bradford lines were laid to a narrower gauge of 4 ft. This was also adopted by the Keighley Tramways Co. Ltd. which, in October 1887, gained the approval of Keighley Corporation to build a system to serve the town. Since most of the directors were also town councillors, the support of the local authority was assured. The authorised capital was £23,000 but only £12,502 was subscribed so the company's ambitions had to be scaled down accordingly.

Horse trams commenced running from North Street, Keighley, to Ingrow on May 8th, 1889, and to Utley on December 18th following. The total length of line was two miles, the track being single with numerous passing places. The trams were of double deck, open top design. The larger ones required two horses but the smaller cars used for off peak traffic could be drawn by a single horse.

The Keighley Tramways Company was not a prosperous concern. It looked to ways of supplementing its income and in 1891 commenced to run a waggonette service. An arrangement was made with the Borough Fire Brigade to allow the tram horses to be borrowed at short notice in case of serious fires. Passengers must have been really impressed on those occasions when their tram was left stranded as the horses galloped off at the head of a fire engine!

By 1894 the financial position was giving cause for concern and the company was unable to meet its obligations to the corporation for road maintenance. On November 25th, 1896, an agreement was signed by which the tram tracks were sold to the Corporation for the nominal sum of £5 and leased back to the company for a period of thirteen years. The days of company operation were now numbered. In 1898, the Corporation obtained an Act authorising the extension and electrification of the tramways. Two years later a municipal electricity works was brought into use. The next step was for the corporation to seek outright control of the tramways and, in December 1900, an offer was made giving the shareholders 11/8d in the £ on their investment. The offer was accepted and ownership passed on September 21st, 1901. The way was now open for Keighley to move into the electric tramway era.

**The electric trams**

In September, 1902, the Corporation was approached by the Mid-Yorkshire Tramways Co. Ltd. which wished to explain its proposal for an electric tramway system centred on Shipley and running to Keighley via Bingley, to Frizinghall, where connection would be made with the Bradford system, and also to Baildon and Ilkley. The company already had the support of Shipley Urban District Council. Keighley insisted that lines within its boundaries should be under corporation and not private ownership and, prompted by the company's initiative, sought Parliamentary powers to construct a line from the junction of North Street and Cavendish Street to the boundary at Stockbridge. The royal assent was received in August 1903. At the same time, Mid-Yorkshire Tramways was authorised to build its line along the main road from Shipley to Stockbridge whence its trams would run over the Keighley Corporation tracks into the town centre. A local service between Keighley and Stockbridge, passing the railway station, was to be operated by the corporation.

The horse trams continued to operate to Ingrow and Utley, but in February 1904 the Corporation resolved to bring these lines within the electrification scheme. To allow for the relaying and doubling of the track, a complete cessation of services was required. The horse tramway was closed on May 28th, 1904.

By this time the Mid-Yorkshire Tramways' scheme had failed

through lack of capital. The only lines built by the company were in Shipley and these were purchased by Bradford Corporation. Keighley now saw less urgency for the Stockbridge line and decided that, initially, the electric trams would run from the railway station to Ingrow and Utley. These services commenced on October 12th, 1904. The station bridge was deemed unsuitable as a terminus and so from the start the trams continued on a single track for a short way to the Victoria Park gates. The distance from there to Stockbridge was only half a mile and it had already been decided that the single track would be extended. Running to Stockbridge commenced on February 10th, 1905. The network now consisted of three routes, each of one mile, centred on the Mechanics Institute at the top of Cavendish Street. The timetable provided a basic service of trams every ten minutes from the Institute to each terminus. Through services operated between all three termini.

Ten open top double deck trams were built to work the services. Two further cars, delivered in 1906, had the advantage of canopies over the top deck. This facility was added to the rest of the fleet in 1910-12.

**Failure to expand and premature closure**

Although proposals were occasionally heard for tramway extension, the Keighley Tramways Department experimented with motor and trolleybus schemes to serve the areas beyond the tram termini. Many of these adventures met with failure. While the residents of the outlying areas sometimes waited in vain for a satisfactory service, the trams demonstrated the reliability of rail transport within the town.

Since 1904, Bradford trams had operated as far as the Shipley/Bingley boundary at Nab Wood. Following negotiations with Bingley Urban District Council, the tracks were extended through Bingley to Crossflatts in 1914. Only two miles, between Crossflatts and Stockbridge, now separated the Bradford and Keighley systems. When the Crossflatts line opened, on October 13th, the First World War had been in progress for two months and further extensions could not be contemplated until peace was restored.

Throughout the war and the period of austerity immediately afterwards, the trams continued to give reliable service whilst that provided by the corporation buses was indifferent. The problem was that the Tramways Department had no funds available for capital expenditure. Not only were new lines out of the question but the Corporation was unwilling to undertake major renewals. that were becoming increasingly urgent within the existing network. The Ministry of Transport declined to ease the responsibilities towards maintaining the roads upon which the tracks were laid.

In May 1923, the Council accepted a Tramways Committee recommendation that the trams should be replaced by trolleybuses as an alternative to heavy expenditure on track relaying. The three lines were closed on different dates to fit in with the introduction of the new trolleybuses. The Utley line closed on August 20th, 1924, and Stockbridge on November 20th. Trams operated from Keighley Station to Ingrow until midday on Wednesday December 17th, 1924. Without ceremony, the trams passed into history. The neighbouring Bradford City Tramways succumbed to a similar fate over the period 1928 to 1950. The line to Crossflatts, which might have become part of a tramway from Bradford to Keighley, survived until May 7th, 1939.

---

## TABLE OF DISTANCES, OPENING AND CLOSURE DATES

Many of the stations listed below were rebuilt or resited during their lives. Most of these changes are mentioned in the text. Some names changed but only by the addition or removal of suffixes. The double names reflect the claim by the Midland Railway to serve additional places which were, in fact, some distance from the railway. Dates marked 'c' are not known exactly. Closure dates are the last day of operation, or in the case of goods lines, the last working day before official closure.

### Leeds to Bradford Forster Square
### Opened, June 30th, 1846

| Miles | Stations | Opened | Closed |
|---|---|---|---|
| 0 | Leeds Wellington | 30.6.1846 | - |
| ½ | Holbeck (Midland) | 2.6.1862 | 5.7.1958 |
| 1¾ | Armley Canal Road | c Sep 1847 | 20.3.1965 |
| 3¼ | Kirkstall | July 1846 | 20.3.1965 |
| 4¼ | Kirkstall Forge | 1.7.1860 | 31.7.1905 |
| 4¾ | Newlay & Horsforth | Sep 1846 | 20.3.1965 |
| 6 | Calverley & Rodley | July 1846 | 20.3.1965 |
| 7¾ | Apperley Bridge & Rawdon | July 1846 | 20.3.1965 |
| 9¼ | Idle | c Sep 1847 | c Sep 1848 |
| 10¾ | Shipley | July 1846 | - |
| 11¾ | Frizinghall | 1.2.1875 | 20.3.1965 |
| 12½ | Manningham | 17.2.1868 | 20.3.1965 |
| 13½ | Bradford Forster Square | 30.6.1846 | - |

## Shipley to Skipton
### Opened Shipley to Keighley, March 16th, 1847
### Keighley to Skipton, September 7th, 1847

| Miles From Leeds | Stations | Opened | Closed |
|---|---|---|---|
| - | Shipley | July 1846 | - |
| 11½ | Saltaire | c May 1856 | 20.3.1965 |
| 13¾ | Bingley | 16.3.1847 | - |
| 16¼ | Thwaites | 1.6.1892 | 30.6.1909 |
| 17 | Keighley | 16.3.1847 | - |
| 20 | Steeton & Silsden | c Dec 1847 | 20.3.1965 |
| 21¾ | Kildwick & Crosshills | Sep 1847 | 21.3.1965 |
| 23 | Cononley | c Dec 1847 | 21.3.1965 |
| 26 | Skipton | 7.9.1847 | - |

## Keighley to Oxenhope
### Opened April 13th, 1867:   Closed June 23rd, 1962:
### Reopened June 29th, 1968

| Miles | Stations | Opened | Closed | Reopened |
|---|---|---|---|---|
| 0 | Keighley | 16.3.1847 | - | - |
| 1¼ | Ingrow | 13.4.1867 | 30.12.1961 | 29.6.1968 |
| 2 | Damems | Sep 1867 | 21.5.1949 | 29.6.1968 |
| 2¾ | Oakworth | 13.4.1867 | 30.12.1961 | 29.6.1968 |
| 3½ | Haworth | 13.4.1867 | 30.12.1961 | 29.6.1968 |
| 4¾ | Oxenhope | 13.4.1867 | 30.12.1961 | 29.6.1968 |

## Bradford Exchange to Halifax and Keighley via Queensbury

| Opened | Goods traffic only | All Traffic |
|---|---|---|
| Bradford Exchange - St. Dunstans | - | 7.1.1867 |
| St. Dunstans - Great Horton | 4.12.1876 ) | |
| Great Horton - Clayton | 9.7.1877 ) | 14.10.1878 |
| Clayton - Thornton | 1.5.1878 ) | |
| Horton Park - City Road | 4.12.1876 | - |
| Queensbury - Holmfield | 14.10.1878 ) | |
| Holmfield - North Bridge | 1.9.1874 ) | 1.12.1879 |
| North Bridge - Halifax | 17.8.1874 ) | |
| Thornton - Denholme | 1.9.1882 | 1.1.1884 |
| Denholme - Ingrow | 1.4.1884 | 7.4.1884 |
| Ingrow - Keighley | 1.4.1884 | 1.11.1884 |

## Closed to all traffic

| | |
|---|---|
| St. Dunstans - Horton Park - City Road | 25.8.1972 |
| Horton Park - Thornton | 25.6.1965 |
| Queensbury - Holmfield | 26.5.1956 |
| Holmfield - North Bridge | 25.6.1960 |
| North Bridge - Halifax | 28.4.1974 |
| Thornton - Cullingworth | 9.11.1963 |
| Cullingworth - Ingrow | 26.5.1956 |
| Ingrow - Keighley | 25.6.1965 |

| Miles | Stations | Opened | Closed |
|---|---|---|---|
| 0 | Bradford Exchange | 9.5.1850 | - |
| ½ | St. Dunstans | cJan. 1879 | 13.9.1952 |
| 1 | Manchester Road | 14.10.1878 | 31.12.1915 |
| 1¾ | Horton Park | 1.11.1880 | 13.9.1952 |
| 2¼ | Great Horton | 14.10.1878 | 21.5.1955 |
| 3½ | Clayton | 14.10.1878 | 21.5.1955 |
| 4½ | Queensbury | 12.4.1879 | 21.5.1955 |
| 6¾ | Holmfield | 15.12.1879 | 21.5.1955 |
| 7¾ | Ovenden | 2.6.1881 | 21.5.1955 |
| 8¾ | North Bridge | 25.3.1880 | 21.5.1955 |
| 9½ | Halifax | 1.7.1844 | - |
| 6 | Thornton | 14.10.1878 | 21.5.1955 |
| 7½ | Denholme | 1.1.1884 | 21.5.1955 |
| 8½ | Wilsden | 1.7.1886 | 21.5.1955 |
| 9¾ | Cullingworth | 7.4.1884 | 21.5.1955 |
| 12¼ | Ingrow (G.N.) | 7.4.1884 | 21.5.1955 |
| 13½ | Keighley | 16.3.1847 | - |

## SOURCES AND BIBLIOGRAPHY

**North of Leeds,** Peter E. Baughan (Roundhouse Books, 1966).

**The Railways of Wharfedale,** Peter E. Baughan (David & Charles, 1969).

**The Lancashire & Yorkshire Railway,** John Marshall (David & Charles, 1969-70).

**Regional History of the Railways of Great Britain, Volume 8: South & West Yorkshire,** David Joy (David & Charles, 1975).

**Keighley Corporation Transport,** Stanley King (Advertiser Press, 1964).

**History of the Keighley & Worth Valley Railway,** Ralph Povey (K.W.V.R.P.S., 1963).

**Railways in Yorkshire, The West Riding,** David Joy (Dalesman Books, 1976).

**Railways in West Yorkshire,** A. Haigh (Dalesman Books, 1974).

**Bradford Tramways,** D.J. Croft (Oakwood Press, 1976).

**Trains Illustrated/Modern Railways.**

**Bradshaw's Railway Guide.**

**Bradford Observer.**

**Telegraph & Argus.**

**Keighley News.**

**Halifax Courier.**